SHe COOKS, He EATS

SHE COOKS, HE EATS

HE EATS

Arlene Krasner
Mark Saunders

knishbooks

San Miguel de Allende, Mexico

Book design by Ray Rhamey

ISBN 978-1-7375155-2-4
Library of Congress Control Number: 2021913728

Cartoons in this book were drawn by Mark Saunders and are from the weekly cartoon panel "The New Epicureans," created by David Boxerman and Mark Saunders. The cartoons are used here by permission of the creators.

Two cannibals were eating a clown.
One turned to the other and said,
"This tastes funny!"

Contents

Amuse-bouche

I'll have to use your coat pocket.
We're no longer putting leftovers
in Styrofoam containers.

Foreword

Okay, we opened with a corny joke, so why stop now. Here's another one.

A doctor tells a group of patients, "What we put into our stomachs is terrible. Red meat is awful. Soft drinks ruin your stomach lining. Fast food is loaded with carcinogens. High-fat diets can be disastrous. And none of us realizes the long-term harm caused by the germs in our drinking water. But there is one thing that is the most dangerous of all. Can anyone here tell me what food it is that causes the most grief and suffering for years after eating it?" An old man raises his hand and says, "Wedding cake."

We've been married for more than 40 years and have put many things in our respective stomachs over those four decades, and much of that input has been delicious, if not incredible. Simply put, we both love food. One enjoys cooking, the other enjoys eating. We're like an extra lyric from the Frank Sinatra song "Love and Marriage," sans horse and carriage.

But all has not been smooth sailing in our kitchen. It has been a marriage with its fair share of food fights. For instance, he can't stand herring and she can't stand shrimp.

The inspiration for our book came out of a conversation we were having one happy hour about food. We enjoyed the conversation and began challenging each other with topics or prompts to answer, and had much fun in the process. In writing this book, we didn't share our respective answers to a specific prompt with each other until the first draft was completed.

Please join us as we share our different perspectives on a series of subjects, our version of a he said-she said conversation centered around food. No pies will be thrown in this food fight, no dishes broken, no expensive Waterford crystal shattered (we don't own any crystal). But we will reveal our likes and dislikes, as well as our reverence for a good meal, by responding separately to the prompts.

Unlike a meal served in courses, there is no sequential order to the food topics we discuss in this book. So, feel free to move around the cabin and, like walking a buffet line, pick and choose the ones you want to read first, second, and so on.

Dinner is now being served. All hail the chef! And don't forget to tip your waitstaff.

L'Aperitif

I gave up eating fish. I'm into tofu.

The Cook

I've always cooked. One of my earliest memories is cooking teeny-tiny hamburgers on the hot radiators in my parent's apartment. Using a teeny-tiny spatula, I flipped burgers to feed to my sister. Meryl would eat anything.

Meryl was everything that I was not. She slept, she smiled, she ate. Boy did she eat. I fed her everything that I didn't want to eat, which was just about everything.

To this day, I feel responsible for her lifetime weight struggle.

My mother was over-protective to a degree that is almost inconceivable. When I begged for a bicycle, she got me a used bike that was kept at my cousin's house. This meant that I could only ride when we went there for a visit—basically we drove so I could ride my bike. And then I was limited to riding around the block.

My mother's over-protectiveness did not—surprisingly— extend to cooking. At six or seven years old, I was reheating dinner for my father and sister when my mother was at work. I gradually eased into cooking some of the dinner.

My father was quite the eater and it wasn't long before my father was requesting some foods directly from me.

One of his favorites was Spaghetti with Butter Sauce. A heart stopper if there ever was one. He remembered it from the Italian family he lived with for a while and asked me to replicate it. It was the first recipe that I ever "made up." Later, it morphed into spaghetti with garlic and olive oil. A bit less of a heart-stopper.

When I moved to Manhattan, I really started learning about foods and cooking. It was the start of the food revolution in New York—soon to be overtaken by the food tidal wave in California—and I wanted to learn everything. I went to all types of restaurants and tried foods that I never heard of before. I ate Mussels Posillipo in Little Italy and Crab Cantonese in Chinatown. I tried French food, Spanish Basque, and Early American food.

And, I cooked. I started reading *Gourmet* magazine and tried recipe after recipe. I made my own bagels—in New York that's like bringing coals to Newcastle—and even made Moo Shu Pork with pancakes. (It took me the better part of a day with the end result of something more akin to Long Island Chinese food than to Chinatown Chinese food. I didn't try to cook another Chinese dish for 40 years!)

On a small street in Greenwich Village, a charcuterie opened. Every Saturday, I'd walk there with Dennis, my white poodle, to get pâté and quiche. Dennis loved quiche and they would give him the "day-old" leftovers. Dennis was quite the gourmet. Now that I knew what pâté tasted like, I started making my own.

Cooks need eaters. Cooks without eaters are like fish without water. I mean, really, where would a cook be without an eater? My dad—and now Mark, my husband—was an eater.

I don't know which parent I am more like when it comes to personality. But they both made me a cook and, eventually, somewhat of an eater.

Actually, I don't behave like either one of them, which is probably why I think I was dropped into the family, fully formed.

The Eater

I say potato chip and Arlene says *potatoes au gratin*. To paraphrase the words of the poet Keats, that is all ye need to know about our personal relationship with food. Well, not quite all. There's more to the story.

Quite frankly, I came late to the *au gratin* party. When I was a kid, I wasn't much of an eater. My mom cooked delicious meals. But food didn't do it for me back then, with the possible exception of candy—and even a kid knows that's not food.

My cooking repertoire was not exactly extensive. As long as we had a gas stove, I could make a grilled cheese sandwich (a slice of American cheese between two pieces of butter-smeared bread) or a grilled hot dog (remove hot dog from fridge, stick on a fork, turn on the stovetop, cook to taste, pretend you are camping). I was committed to comic books and sports and fishing and drawing and Saturday morning TV Westerns and cartoons; I also did a lot of reading, and, for a brief time, my two favorite books were *The Lives of the Saints* and *Mad Magazine*, which probably explains why I'm still so neurotic.

I wasn't a fussy eater, as much as I just wasn't much of an eater. All that changed in high school. I attended a public high school, after having gone to Catholic schools for my earlier education. During the first week, I had to get weighed for gym class. I checked in at all of 79 pounds in my skivvies, which basically meant, as a shy and small kid from a private school, I had a "kick me" sign virtually taped to my back. To this day, I consider not getting stuffed in a locker to be the crowning achievement of my freshman year of high school.

Feeling under-sized, and rightly so since I was, I appealed to my parents to get me a doctor's prescription that would excuse me from P.E. As an asthmatic, I found the gym classes, from weight-lifting to swimming to long-distance running, to be grueling. In my mind, I had a fair shot at getting a doctor's excuse.

But the doctor thought otherwise and sold me out. Like Pat O'Brien calling James Cagney a coward in the movie *The Fighting 69th* and telling him to quit whining and get out there and join the others in the trenches, the doctor told me exercise would be the best thing for my lungs. He was right, of course. If you can't beat 'em, join 'em. So, my parents bought me a set of weights, and I put on twenty pounds of mostly muscle for my sophomore year. I tried out for the high school wrestling team and made the varsity.

That's when food for me became an obsession.

My senior year I lost twenty pounds to make a specific weight class. For a time, I limited myself to 500 calories a day, which is close to starving for a growing teen. The unintended consequence of this weight loss was a sense of food insecurity, which I carried with me, mostly in my head and around my waist, for a very long time.

After I graduated high school, my parents moved to Reno, Nevada, and I followed along. For my first six months there, I worked a full-time swing shift—3 P.M. to 11 P.M.—at the Mapes Hotel restaurant in downtown Reno. It was my introduction to pecan pie; one of the waitresses would, on occasion, intentionally ruin a slice of pie and give it to me. They also made a delicious hot turkey open-faced sandwich, with mashed potatoes and gravy. I ate well. Pecan pie remains one of my special desserts. Most notably while working there, I once served coffee to one of the Lombardo brothers (Guy, I think), not to mention coffee to Lorenzo St. DuBois (Dick Shawn). While at the Mapes, I didn't just re-fill the coffee mugs of the rich and famous, I put on the twenty pounds I had lost in high school and then some.

Post-college, I joined the U.S. Navy, where during my active duty I worked as a journalist assigned to the Seabees, the Navy's version of the Army Corps of Engineers. Picture, if you will, dining with construction workers with huge appetites being served four big meals a day; I gained another twenty-pounds-plus while in the Navy.

Today, I am twice the man I once was—in girth. Buda boom. I'm 200 pounds, which means I swallowed that 79-pound kid a long time ago. I didn't get here overnight, however. I largely—pun intended--measure my life by the

great meals I've enjoyed. And there have been many, especially since meeting Arlene.

We met in a small university English department,
where we both taught Freshman Composition. Along with
six other graduate students, we shared a bullpen-like office
space. Every day, Arlene and I would get coffee together in
the morning and lunch in the afternoon and enjoyed each
other's company. We talked often. We became close enough
for Arlene to invite me to her house one evening for dinner.
She made a spinach salad with a tangy olive oil and vinegar
dressing, a few bacon bits and blue cheese crumbles, as I
recall, as well as croutons, and fettuccine alfredo with garlic
bread.

I moved in the next day.

A Meal for the End of the World or What I Ate During the Pandemic

The Cook

Did you see the movie *Desperately Seeking a Friend for the End of the World?* Basically, a huge meteor—or something like that—is headed for Earth and will destroy us. All attempts to destroy the meteor or push it off-course have failed.

I found the movie very depressing, but thought-provoking. What would my last meal be and who would I invite?

I don't think I'd have one last meal; I'd have many last meals. Top of my list is herring in cream sauce. I don't eat herring very often and always opt for the less fattening, healthier pickled version. Now, since it would be a last meal, albeit one of many, I wouldn't have any cholesterol worries so I'd go for the cream sauce. I'd eat it every day for breakfast and maybe even happy hour with a very dry martini, or two.

Foie Gras: As much of it as I could possibly eat, in as many ways as I could possibly prepare it. Lamb, in every way imaginable.

And lobster, the more lobster the better. I love lobster rolls, so I could have that for lunch. A good follow-on from my breakfast herring.

And cake—chocolate cake—lots of it. And Crème Brûlée, maybe some Tiramisù as a chaser.

I would want to share all this with Mark, my husband, of course. But who else?

I would want to gather all my friends to one place so we could spend the last days together eating and drinking. We would sit around and tell funny stories and eat and then tell more funny stories. It would be an endless dinner party—until the meteor struck and the party ended.

The best thing is that I could make a massive mess in the kitchen and not have to worry about it. That would be a good thing.

What do my friends want for their last meal? Mary wants red beans and rice, with cornbread and butter and lemon pie. David wants pound cake with fresh blueberries and vanilla ice cream, followed by watermelon. Mark—ever the gourmet—wants lamb chops and potatoes au gratin. Dennis, on the other hand, goes the comfort route with meatloaf. One friend, who shall remain nameless, wants Ecstasy.

Me? I'm sticking with lobster. And herring. And lots of pot edibles to keep my spirits up.

As I write this now, it is 2021 and we are in the middle of a pandemic. I never really thought about a pandemic. I mean, really, who ever really did except for some health professionals whose job it is to think about such things. But well, in 2021, here we are, isolating at home and cooking whatever we find at the market, or in our pantry and freezer.

This is not exactly what I had in mind when I thought about my last meal when a meteor hits the earth and obliterates all of us. This has been more insidious—isolating us from others, causing hoarding of foods and necessities. Will we ever forget the Great Toilet Paper Shortage?

People who have barely opened a can are now cooking, or trying to cook, full meals. Many restaurants are closed; but there's still take-out and curbside pickup. You eat alone, or with your self-isolating significant other. You don't want to, or can't, go out to the grocery store often.

So, what do you do? Plan your meals, use your pantry, use your freezer.

As an introvert, a planner, and a cook, I have been practicing for this all my life. I have cooked so much food that we are leaving food gifts at a friend's door. Yes, keeping a safe distance, wiping down containers and taking care with the food.

So far, this week, I made a huge, and I mean huge, amount of granola. I made so much that I've gifted two sets of friends with some. We are trying to devour the rest.

I have also made lots of chicken enchiladas and chicken pot pies. Again, gifting some. My freezer is so full that I have no room for them.

Today, as I write this, I am making a ham. Yes, two people and a ham. Someone's idea of eternity. Tomorrow, it is Split Pea soup with a ham bone. Followed by lasagna. Then leftovers. Whew!

We've made a calendar with the meals to be made on each day. I cook a bunch of stuff on one day, eat some, and freeze the rest. I tend to cook in spurts of geography. We had a week of Soy and Ginger, followed by an Italian weekend, then by Mexican week. I am working up to Greek (lamb!) and, if this self-isolation lasts too long, who knows where we will go.

And still, I don't know what to eat for lunch.

Of course, all this cooking must fit in with our ever-expanding Skype and Zoom events with friends who are also self-isolating.

I have never been as busy as I am now. And I've never socialized as much as I do now.

The Eater

I would like to respond to the second part of the prompt first. I ate well during the pandemic, thank you for asking, and thank you, Arlene, for cooking. Now, instead of focusing on a deadly virus or a gigantic asteroid striking our planet during which said cataclysmic event Hollywood, sadly, is unable to save us, even with overpaid A-list actors, I'm going to discuss this topic from the angle of a well-established and more down-to-earth trope: My last meal.

The concept of a condemned man eating a hearty last meal never quite worked for me. If I were facing execution, I wouldn't exactly have much of an appetite, quite frankly, and I would need to change my underwear every ten minutes. I would probably be queasy and have to be sedated, maybe even pumped full of THC and laughing gas. I suspect they would have to feed my last meal to me through a tube.

Or, better still, perhaps I'd just keep drinking. Now, there's a thought I could live with and die from, although long-term damage to my liver would not be a problem, if I'm facing my last meal. I'd select a range of expensive red wines, perhaps starting with a bottle of Chateau Lafite 1787, from Thomas Jefferson's cellar and valued at over $150,000. Unfortunately, man cannot live by wine alone and, truth be told, drinking is not eating, regardless of what my Uncle Phil thought, may he rest in peace, but that answer does not address the question put forth.

All of which is a round-about way of saying if I had to choose a last meal, I'm thinking of two options. My first option would be to sit down at an all you-can-eat buffet in a Las Vegas casino and bloody well take my bloody time. I might even prolong the evening by playing Keno while eating and throw in a nap or two, which would be mandatory because of my shifting blood sugar levels. That's option #1.

Option #2 would be to attend a Bedouin wedding feast. Officially, such a feast is considered the largest meal in the world and has been whimsically called "camel Turducken." According to Guinness Book of Records a whole camel is stuffed with two sheep, or lambs, which, in turn, are stuffed with around twenty chickens that, in turn, are stuffed with fish. Yummy. On second thought, I'd rather shoot myself on an empty stomach than eat any part of a stuffed camel, and I don't care what or who it has been stuffed with.

Having rejected options 1 and 2, I'm back to square one—or square last. What will I order for my final meal on this planet?

Obviously, I would want my favorite cook, Arlene, to prepare and serve my final meal. Just as obviously, I would ask her to make my favorite dish, Spaghetti Carbonara. She makes it for me once a year, on my birthday. If she made it any more than that, one of those delicious bonus meals would be my last, forget the late-to-the-party asteroid. Every year—not on my birthday but on New Year's Eve—I vow to reduce my carbonara footprint. So far, no luck. Her carbonara doth murder diets.

But I'm not going to underachieve and begin and end with only a pasta course. I'm going all-in on gluttony and planning a full evening.

Before I sat down for my last meal, for instance, I would work the room, Negroni in hand, and visit friends for a farewell-bon voyage moment, noshing from plates some underpaid staffer would be carrying around the room, including such favorite Arlene quick bites as potato knishes, pepperoni rolls, gougères (French cheese puffs), and deviled eggs (hers are the best).

With such limited time left and wanting to squeeze every last second out of it, I would expand the dinner menu and surround my carbonara with other delights. The table would be set country-style, with all the food placed on the table at the same time to resemble a potluck, because I know how much Arlene hates potlucks (sorry, dear).

Maestro, music please, as I introduce the menu for my last meal:

Starter course: Scallops. This is a recipe Arlene picked up from one of our favorite Portland restaurants, Andina, which is Peruvian. Two scallops are pan fried and drizzled with maple syrup. The dish is topped with a crown of fried shallots and it is fabulous.

Soup course: Pozole. I'm a late convert to the pozole fan club. Arlene made it for the first time the third time we lived here. Wow. All I can say is, wow. It's a traditional ancient Mexican soup or stew, and that simple description does not do it justice. Calling pozole a soup is like calling a Tesla a car. I know some out there would question my choice, especially since pozole, unlike, say, chicken noodle soup or any gazpacho, can be filling. But it's my last meal, not yours, so back off.

Pasta course: Spaghetti carbonara. I could sing for days and write for months about my love of Arlene's Spaghetti carbonara, in true poetic fashion, my "Ode to Carbonara." Her version is fairly close to the classic Italian version. She adds a dash of cream, which is considered by some traditional chefs to be a mortal sin—gasp! The horror, the horror! But I love her dish, so go ahead and call me a sinner. Just don't call me late for dinner.

Poultry course: Coq au Vin. This is one of my favorite winter dishes Arlene makes, along with her Cassoulet. I know both are considered peasant dishes but, hey, have you gotten a good look at me?

Fish course: Oregon Dungeness Crab. Whenever anyone asks me what food I most miss, living as I do in the middle of Mexico, my answer is always the same: fresh Dungeness Crab from the cold waters of the Pacific Northwest. Period. No qualifications. If you've ever had it, you'd understand.

Vegetable course: I like many vegetables and prefer them simply prepared. No rich sauces or deep-fried coverings or towers in the shape of the Empire State Building. My favorite is, perhaps, asparagus, so any non-fussy asparagus dish would work fine here. I also like zucchini. We used to grow it in our backyard, and it would proliferate like a weed. We had zucchini from summer through the fall. I'm also fond of green beans. Brussels sprouts, anyone? Surprise me.

Meat course: Lamb chops. I know many would pick a nice juicy steak, perhaps a rib-eye or some kind of Wagyu beef cut, for their last meal. But, for my money, the best cooked lamb chops or even the more upscale rack of lamb can take a meat course to a higher level. And I don't even need mint jelly.

Salad course: Small, mixed green salad with blue cheese crumbles (fully dressed, because, hey I'm not planning on saving any of this food), walnuts, and croutons.

Cheese plate: I'll go the easy route here, after all, by this time I am stuffed to Charlie the Tuna's gills, and pick a French brie, a Spanish Manchego, and a blue cheese or cheddar from Rogue Creamery (Go, Oregon!)

Dessert: I had a serious sweet tooth as a kid. "How serious was your sweet tooth?" shouts someone from the back of the room. If I kept eating desserts, I'd only have one tooth left by now and it would be called my sweet tooth. These days, I try to limit my dessert consumption. That said, Arlene makes two wonderful desserts that are both delicious yet light: Pavlova and Grand Marnier® Souffle. Either would work.

Coffee: Very strong Turkish coffee, perhaps whatever was left over from that wedding in the desert. I'd want to stay awake as long as I can in the afterlife. Or, maybe not, depending on where I land. And if I'm asking Arlene to cook all of the above courses for me, I have a good idea where I'm ultimately headed. I'll be the one wearing the Tommy Bahama shirt and flip-flops. It's going to be hot.

What I Eat When I Eat Alone

I will have the hors d'oeuvre du jour, the soup
du jour, the piece de resistance du jour,and the
crème de la crème du jour.

The Cook

I know that there are lots of people who live alone and eat alone all the time. To those people, I apologize for making a somewhat big deal about eating alone. At one time, my sister said to me, "When the kids are gone and Ron and I are alone, I'm not going to cook anymore. It doesn't make sense to cook for only two people."

"But Mark and I are only two people and I cook all the time," I answered.

"You like to cook," she replied.

I know that as one of a two-some, I find some joy in being alone and eating alone. Whenever Mark is gone, I plan my meals so that I eat the foods that he doesn't like. I also don't cook. Yes, that is true. I don't cook—I buy prepared foods, dine out, or graze while he is gone.

One thing that I always turn to when I'm alone is herring. As I write this, I can almost taste it. I love herring in every way: In wine sauce, in cream sauce, rolled up. Every which way you could think of. When I was young, I would watch my father eat lox and herring and whitefish. (Not all at the same time.) I was appalled! How could he eat so much dead fish?

And now, I love herring. How much life changes and surprises us!

I always try to buy *dolmas*—cold rice wrapped in grape leaves—when eating alone. I could eat quite a few before I got tired of them.

Sometimes when I know I'll be alone, I make a pot of ratatouille. I could eat it for lunch and dinner for days on end. I especially love it on an English muffin, with some cheese melted over it. An instant pizza.

But most of all, I like to eat bits and pieces of things when I'm alone. Not exactly cooking, but creating a meal out of what's around.

Mark, who almost never cooks for us, always cooks for himself when I'm not around. Odd.

My friend, Diana, who lives alone and eats alone a lot of the time, cooks for herself just about every day. During the summer months, she grows tons (I mean that literally) of basil and cooks it on pasta with tomatoes or puts it in caprese salads.

In San Francisco, after I left my first husband and was alone, I hardly ever cooked. I heated tortillas over the flame of my gas stove and then slathered butter on them and rolled them up. Yummy! I also ate cheese with good bread every Friday night with my dog, Dennis. That was quite the treat for both of us.

In Reno, I often bought a jar of caviar (a very dusty jar!) and ate it with my cat, Lorraine. We were in heaven!

I guess I don't really eat alone; I always eat with my pets.

But life changes. I have no pets now and I'm hardly ever alone, especially during the pandemic. Mark and I are not traveling—together or separately—and we are not dining with others much. Separately that is. Nor together, actually.

So, I am out of practice eating alone. We eat breakfast together, but make our own. Mark cooks eggs for himself, while I toast an English muffin or a slice of bread. Sometimes, I actually have herring. Mark won't look at my plate, but I'm in heaven.

It is as close to eating alone as someone can be and still feel connected.

The Eater

So, what do I eat when I eat alone? Leftovers. That was easy. Next question? Okay, you in the back of the room with your hand up, the reporter from the Grilled Gizzard Gazette ("All the roadkill that's fit to eat"). Hmm. Yes, I would be glad to expand on my answer.

Although I prefer to eat with Arlene, I actually don't mind eating alone occasionally. Mostly, because I'll be sitting in front of the television set and either watching a movie or sports. Or, if I'm on the road and dining alone at a restaurant, I am likely reading a book. Arlene and I prefer to sit at our dining table, eat, drink, and engage in conversation, throwing off witty one-liners as if we're part of the Algonquin Round Table. Okay, maybe that Algonquin reference is a stretch; sometimes we don't say anything.

My larger point is when it's just the two of us, we rarely eat in front of the TV and, if and when we do, it's only for special occasions. For example, we both loved watching *The Sopranos*, which in its original run aired on Sunday nights. Arlene would make an Italian dish for dinner that evening, and we would sit in front of the TV and watch Tony and his family take on the world or at least New Jersey. In season 2,

Tony found himself in a power struggle with Richie Aprile, recently released from prison. The entire season, as I recall, was building up to a classic showdown between the two men. To deepen the tension and raise the stakes, Richie became engaged to Janice, Tony's sister.

Spoiler alert! In the penultimate (love that word) episode of season 2, Richie and Janice share an intimate dinner at home, in their small kitchen. Always a class act, Richie tells Janice to get them another bottle of wine (I may be off on the details here). She tells him to get it himself, and Richie, not known for his easy-going nature or gentlemanly manner, slaps her. Janice leaves the room to get the wine and returns with a gun and kills Richie. As if on cue, we both jumped up from the sofa and said "Whoa" or something as instinctively profound, almost knocking over our dinner trays. We weren't expecting Richie to get his ticket punched until the next week—and by Tony, not Janice.

But those TV dinner delights are few and far between. As a kid, my family didn't sit in front of the television set and eat dinner (Arlene's family didn't, either). We always ate at the dining room table and, invariably, we always had guests joining us for dinner. It was informal. It was conversational. And it was very Catholic; we couldn't touch our food until someone said a prayer, and we could not eat meat on Fridays. Then, of course, all that changed. Suddenly, hamburgers were in on Friday and fish sticks were out. In spite of what was being served, we always had bread and a salad.

Although I grew up during the Great Frozen Age of Swanson, I don't recall much in the way of eating a TV dinner until my college years. Then, again, I wouldn't recommend much of what I ate in college to a hungry dog.

Today, if back in the USA and eating alone—assuming a frantic search uncovered nothing appealing in the fridge—I'll drive to either KFC or Taco Bell and dine on what is universally considered one of the greatest health threats to Americans: fast food. Damn the carcinogens and full-saturated fat ahead. I may indulge in a small pizza, as long as it's like a New York City slice. Or order in Chinese food. Or order in the latest haute cuisine from Fiji. Anything from anywhere to keep me out of the kitchen.

When all else fails, there's the Seinfeld formula for dinner alone: dry cereal.

Here in San Miguel, it's easier and almost cheaper to go to a neighborhood café or order in when dining alone. It's not as if I can't cook or won't cook, it's just that my culinary portfolio is embarrassingly small, and since Arlene is an amazing cook—and I'm lazy —I gladly defer to her advanced skill set. My cooking skills are better suited for camping in the wild when your choice is binary: eat or get eaten. Sure, I can cook eggs, bacon, hamburgers, hot dogs, and the like. Big deal. Yawn.

When eating alone, I pay due homage to the Great God of Snacks. I'm happy to plow my way through a bowl of bar mix or popcorn or kettle chips. My favorite guilty pleasure, however, is fried pork rinds. When we decided to move to

Mexico, I looked forward to the move for many reasons. Arlene and I both talked about our new exciting adventure south of the border. I never confided in her how excited I was to be living in a country where the national food is fried pork rinds. It's a snack I would always bring with me to poker games, and, conversely, one that is not allowed in our kitchen. Sometimes I might snack on, dare I say, healthy food. Bananas, for instance, are a favorite mid-day nosh. As a kid, I would take a celery stick and fill it with peanut butter for a quick bite. But I haven't done that since, well, since I was a kid. So, yes, mostly my snacks these days are unhealthy and best avoided.

Quite frankly, at this point in my life, I'd rather not eat alone. When and if I find myself in that situation, I shall search high and low for leftovers. Whatever Arlene made weeks ago will always be better than what I could make any day of the week. I guess that's why I'm the designated eater in our family and not the cook.

What I've Learned from Cooking Shows

I'm beginning to really hate these
cookbook tours.

The Cook

I have always thought of myself as a somewhat competitive person. Not overtly competitive. And really not competitive with others, just with myself. I need to be the best I can be and yet not destroy someone else. As I age, I don't really believe any of this. I am really not competitive at all. I just like to win.

I don't know when I started watching cooking shows, but I know that I really got on board with them when I retired in 2005. Food Network started in 1993 and I watched a couple of shows—*Ready, Set, Cook* and *Emeril*, mainly. *Ready, Set, Cook* was probably the first competitive cooking show that debuted on the Food Network in 1995. Emeril Lagasse dominated the network from 1997 to 2007.

I really never watched Julia Child on television. I read her cookbooks and learned how to cook from them, trying more and more complicated recipes. I catered many dinner parties in Reno using her recipes and she never failed me. Her recipes were so good that you could leave out an ingredient and the dish still came out delicious.

Food Network began to change from watching a talented chef cook to watching cooks competing in a variety of shows (*Chopped*, anyone?).

I learned a great deal about cooking from these shows. I watched Ina Garten religiously, Anne Burrell, even Giada (although she is too thin to be taken very seriously). I collected recipes from Ina, and some great cooking tips from Anne.

From the competition shows, I learned some techniques, some no-no's (don't use truffle oil in a competition), some tips (from Bobby Flay: always take some fluffy bread out before making a sandwich). I also learned—mainly from *Chopped*—how to talk about food and how to balance sweet and savory, adding a bit of acid (who knew lemon was so important). I also learned that texture is very important—how to add a bit of crunch to a dish. Pine nuts, anyone?

Chopped has given many chefs the chance to show their skills, increase their worth in the restaurant world. It is now—or should be—common knowledge that many, if not most, chefs are underpaid and have few employee benefits. Yes, many celebrity chefs are bringing in the big bucks, but they supplement their income and bring customers in to their restaurants by being the judges on these shows. A chef who wins a competition can become a celebrity chef and can leave the stove behind. It is really difficult to imagine a chef at 70 or 80 working hunched over a stove. That's for cooks, not chefs. (I don't even want to go into, or think about, when a cook becomes a chef.)

But what about those of us who watch these shows?

I, for one, am tired of them. Cooking is not a competition. It is a means to getting food on the table. I invite people to my table, to my cooking for not only nourishment but for companionship, for love. The food has to be edible, for sure. I don't need to jump through chefy hoops to prepare a meal. Simple is good. The company is the best part of having friends over for a meal. The food, I have to say, is secondary.

I cook almost every day. I do not cook meals that "knock it out of the park" very often during the week. Maybe once a week I manage to do an above average meal.

I've read that these cooking shows have caused many (mostly men, I think) to create their own cooking competitions. I cannot think of anything less enticing than watching some guy, who cooks only on the weekend, if that, cook with very expensive ingredients to wow his guests. Look at me!

The real winner—male or female—is the person who cooks day in and day out, trying to make meals that are nourishing, interesting, and flavorful. It is not cooking everyday meals that is difficult; it is the planning, the shopping, the cleanup that is difficult. I think almost anyone who cooks once every two or three weeks, or months, can do a very creditable job. Just try doing it every day!

When I read food memoirs, I am reminded about how the simplest meals evoke the best memories. I remember reading M.F.K. Fisher describing cooking freshly shucked peas in the garden. I could picture the scene, taste the peas, relive the memory even though it isn't my memory. Does it get any simpler than cooking fresh peas with people you love?

No competition there.

I do have to say that my cooking has improved since watching these shows. Actually, my cooking hasn't improved as much as Mark now understands why I do the things I do. He is more a partner in my cooking than ever before. And he now cooks more than before. He will add sriracha to his scrambled eggs, as well as pine nuts or walnuts added to salads or sprinkled over a dish. He understands that cooking takes time and patience and attention.

So, thank you, Cooking Shows, for making cooks more appreciated.

The Eater

My full appreciation of cooking shows began with a death. On August 13, 2004, culinary legend Julia Child died peacefully in her sleep. She was 91. Arlene and other friends came up with the idea to have a special dinner in honor of Julia. Ten of us participated. The theme for our first dinner--a memorial to Julia—was French, of course, with all recipes coming from her book *Mastering the Art of French Cooking*. We ran her cooking shows in a loop on a TV in the background; we also ran Dan Aykroyd's unforgettable parody of her cooking show.

The group formally dressed up for the occasion, and we all ate well. Very well, indeed, since everyone in the group was a food enthusiast and dead-serious about the food they serve to others, as well as the wine or cocktails selected to accompany their course. I was one of only two unofficial designated eaters. The rest of the group owned shelves of cook books and could recite favorite recipes by memory. The evening was delightful. We decided to continue meeting for dinners as a group and branded ourselves "The Julia Child Supper Club" (JCSC).

Our JCSC rules were simple. As a group, we would decide the next cuisine, ultimately covering food from a range of cultures, including French, Italian, German, Peruvian, Mexican, Chinese, Scandinavian, East Indian, and Native American, to name but a few. Each household would host a dinner, and we would meet approximately once every three months. The host would provide the entrée, with the rest signing up for the other courses.

Arlene and I always seemed to bring together like-minded food lovers for dinner. Long before we helped to start the Julia Child Supper Club, we had formed a dining group consisting of high-tech co-workers. Everyone in the group worked long hours during the week, so most of our dining out together took place over the weekend.

It once took us two and a half hours of driving, one-way, from our home in Portland, Oregon, to Oyster Bay, Washington, for a group Sunday brunch at The Ark. One couple flew their private plane to the brunch. Not to be outdone, we drove our new car: a Yugo. For those who don't remember, a Yugo was the cheapest new car in America and still over-priced. In the movie remake of *Dragnet*, one of the characters said the Yugo was on the cutting edge of Serbo-Croatian technology. When we bought the car, they gave us a tee-shirt that said: "Wherever I go. Yugo." Five hours in the Yugo gave us enough time to stress-test that vehicle. We got rid of the car a few months later and kept the shirt. The jokes wrote themselves. What do you call a Yugo with a flat tire? Totaled. What do you call passengers in a Yugo? Shock absorbers. How do you make a Yugo go faster? Get it towed. Although the jokes didn't write themselves, I didn't write them. Someone else did. I mention the brunch because the restaurant was recommended by James Beard, who considered The Ark his favorite seafood spot, and he was besties with Julia Child.

Wait a minute. What does any of this have to do with cooking shows? It's complicated. Arlene and I didn't start watching televised cooking shows on a regular basis until we both retired. Before retirement, we would occasionally catch a food show together. In addition to watching Julia Child re-runs, I remember programs such as *The Galloping Gourmet*, long since having galloped off into the sunset. But once we retired and discovered the joys of having time to waste sitting mindlessly in front of a TV screen, we began watching more cooking shows.

I recall early Food Network shows, such as *Ready, Set, Cook* and *Emeril Live* and *Iron Chef*. What started with chefs teaching home cooks how to make specific dishes (fill in the blank here with just about anything by food-loving cooks, from Julia Child to Ina Garten), eventually morphed into cooking competitions, such as *Chopped, Hell's Kitchen, Top Chef, Master Chef*, etc. I confess to enjoying the competitive cooking shows. One sad lesson learned from watching all these shows, however, is realizing how little money most professional chefs make in their day-to-day job. When a chef wins the $10,000 prize on *Chopped*, it's often life-changing.

Of course, all food shows are not competitions. Anything by Anthony Bourdain is worth watching. We watched *High on the Hog* on Netflix, about the impact of African-American cuisine and totally enjoyed it, learning a lot along the way. Without the African influence, there's a good chance Southern U.S. cuisine today would be identified mostly as deep-fried haggis and cabbage. Then there was *Salt Fat Acid Heat* by Samin Nosrat, based on her book, a fascinating look at four elements of cooking one must master. And I can't continue without mentioning one of my favorite food shows: *Somebody Feed Phil*. As an eater, I truly relate to Phil's unbridled enthusiasm whenever he tastes something great; when he does, he breaks out in his own trademark dance, throwing his arms wildly in the air, shaking and smiling. Hallelujah! Praise the cook and pass the plate.

I know the feeling.

Truth be told, I didn't have to watch any cooking shows on television to learn about food. I live in a show. Arlene has an enormous cook book collection, and had more than a decade's worth of printed cooking magazines, especially *Gourmet* and *Bon Appétit*. Arlene still loves trying out new recipes, and I love eating. Need I say more?

Okay, so what did I learn from watching all these cooking shows? Plenty. To appear more food-savvy, I learned to talk about a dish having a flavor profile or being succulent or nutty or sublime. I no longer mention steak or chicken, which sounds uncouth or insufficient; instead, I have upgraded those food items to "proteins." I learned you don't mix cheese with fish. I try not to overuse such words as "decadent" or "sinful" or "to die for" when discussing dessert. I learned that whatever you do in a competition judged by chefs, you never use white Truffle oil. I learned when you compete against Bobby Flay, you don't pick a dish from the American Southwest as your signature dish. If you do, you'll lose. Or, if your signature dish somehow involves bread, such as a Po'Boy sandwich, remember to scoop out most of the bread before adding the good stuff and serving. Mr. Flay always removes some of the bread, and he always wins those particular challenges. And why not? He's been with the Food Network since 1995.

If I were to go head-to-head with Bobby Flay, I already know my signature dish: Parmesan Crisps. For those unfamiliar with the dish, a chimpanzee could make it, as long as the chimp could set and read a kitchen timer or otherwise notice when the crisps were done. A crisp is nothing more than a spoonful of grated parmesan placed in the shape of a small mound (think volcano cone) on a baking sheet. The parmesan is baked in the oven at 350-degrees for ten minutes, give or take, where it spreads out to create a wafer-thin cracker. The dish couldn't be any simpler and it's been my go-to appetizer for years.

Based on that one dish, people who don't really know me think I can cook. I doubt I'll be able to fool Bobby Flay.

A Nostalgia Meal

The Cook

I am not a sentimental person. I do not hold on to trinkets, looking longingly at them for hours. I am not a pack rat.

But still, a meal from my past does bring a bit of longing to my heart. Of course, considering that my grandmother was a horrid cook and my mother disavowed any knowledge of Jewish cooking, my sentimental meal is a combination of what might have been and what was.

I don't know if it counts as a nostalgic meal, but I love herring in any way, with any kind of sauce. No one I know likes herring as much as I do. Well, maybe my friend Herje, but he is Swedish and it is in his blood. Even here, in the middle of Mexico, I sometimes find and buy a jar of pickled herring and eat the whole jar myself. I have to since I have no one to share it with.

My mother was very nostalgic for mamaliga, which is basically polenta for the Romanian peasants. She often spoke of her father stirring the cornmeal and making quite a show of it. She never made it for us, probably because it was peasant food and she had risen above that level.

A nostalgic meal would be very difficult—but not impossible—to pull off. You would have to invite others who shared your food history.

Rather than use nationality—of whatever persuasion—you could use time. For example, have a retro 1950s cocktail party. You could make martinis or manhattans, pigs in a blanket, angels on horseback (oysters wrapped in bacon), devils on horseback (dates wrapped in bacon), or rumaki, which for those too young to know, consists of water chestnuts and pieces of duck or chicken liver wrapped in bacon and marinated in soy sauce with ginger or brown sugar.

Back then, we obviously wrapped everything in bacon, which may account for our later cholesterol problems.

Some nostalgic meals can transcend both time and place. These are meals that evoke a feeling, such as the first date with a long-time lover. I think Mark feels that way about Fettuccine Alfredo and Spinach salad, which I made for him when we started dating. I don't think I've ever made it again. Why mess with a great memory?

Sometimes it is not the meal that we're nostalgic for but the time of our life. When I was a graduate student in Reno, Nevada, I would drive to the store for cheap, jarred caviar. It wasn't the caviar I wanted; it was the semblance of a former life of culture.

When Mark and I left graduate school, and Reno, for our yet unknown careers in California, we were poorer than we were in graduate school. I developed a dish that I called Stuffed Shells. It was pasta—the shells—with ground meat (one pound), jarred spaghetti sauce, and some cheese. I boiled the pasta, browned the meat, then mixed everything together and baked until the cheese melted.

We ate it for four or five days. I never made it again.

The Eater

A nostalgia meal? May I have that in a sentence, please? Never mind. I think I understand the prompt. You want to know what meal I think of fondly, and whenever I eat the same meal, I'm transported in time back to happier days? Like Proust eating a madeleine or that chubby kid in *Stand by Me* eating one more pie.

My memory is faulty these days and, truth be told, always has been. With two odd exceptions: I can recall meals I've consumed, and I can recall scenes and dialogue from books and movies. Some communities measure their history with categories of great significance: The Year of the Big Flood; The Year of the Great Fire; The Year of the Violent Earthquake. My life measurements tend to center around food. For instance, one category in my life might be "The Night I Ate Monk Fish Bathed in a Rich Lobster Sauce for the First Time."

Let's start with my monk fish meal. Arlene and I were in San Francisco for a computer conference. We were planning to go to Fisherman's Wharf for dinner one evening, but were exhausted from spending all day at the conference. We were staying at the elegant Miyako Hotel in an area known as Japan Town, and noticed a positive review on a wall for their own hotel restaurant. Not ones to waste a good restaurant review, we decided to eat in the hotel that evening. Before then, I had never even heard of monk fish--what I have since learned is it is known as a poor man's lobster. I tasted my first bite and softly muttered "Hmm." I took a second bite and released another "Hmm." A third taste elicited the same response, at which point Arlene asked what I was doing. I bravely threw the question back at her and asked what do you mean what am I doing? She said every time I took a bite, I let out a sound. Honestly, I didn't even know I was saying all those "Hmms." Our dinner at the Miyako Hotel was memorable but not a legitimate candidate for a nostalgic meal. So, eighty-six the monk fish.

A meal that clearly would qualify is what Arlene calls stuffed shells. It is a cheap pasta meal that features ground beef as its, ahem, protein. When we left graduate school, we moved to a bedroom community in the Redwood Empire, near Santa Rosa, California. Keeping with a food-theme, we had moved from Reno to our new location in a Keebler Cookie truck, owned by a friend of my father's. We arrived just in time for a recession and had a difficult time finding meaningful full-time employment. Make that any employment, even of the meaningless variety. To save money, Arlene would make "stuffed shells" and we'd eat it three or four nights a week. Upon reflection, forget I even mentioned that pasta dish. The memory it conjures is not a happy one, and a nostalgia meal should evoke positive memories. Am I right?

By far, our favorite U.S. city is New York City. Arlene is originally from Long Beach, Long Island, but has been out West for more than 40 years. We try to visit the Big Apple every couple of years, and when we do, it seems we always have a nostalgia meal. Arlene attended NYU and worked there, as well. Gran Ticino was her favorite neighborhood restaurant in the Village, and we'd always have at least one meal there. Gran Ticino, you might recall, was a restaurant made famous in the movie *Moonstruck*, written by playwright John Patrick Shanley; it's where Johnny Cammareri (Danny Aiello) proposed to Loretta Castorini (Cher). Shanley attended NYU and the original Gran Ticino was a popular student and faculty hangout. Unfortunately, the restaurant closed its doors after nearly 90 years of being in business, just one of the many casualties of the tragedy of 9/11.

Whenever we visit New York these days, we start with a different nostalgia meal. Our first meal in Manhattan is always at Becco on Restaurant Row, walking distance to Broadway. Becco serves regional Italian food and is part of the famous Bastianich family of Italian restauranteurs. It is perhaps best known for its unlimited pasta; you may choose as many servings of three daily special pastas as you can eat. Becco is also known for its wide selection of Italian wines, all priced at $35 a bottle. A steal anywhere, especially in New York. We usually start with a glass of prosecco, order an antipasti plate, which includes an assortment of marinated and grilled vegetables and seafood, and then move on to their unlimited pasta. Becco is tasty and lively and friendly and always brings back good memories of our previous visits to New York. It's certainly not a fancy restaurant or perhaps even your best dining option in a city known for offering thousands. Nonetheless, I look forward to our next trip to Manhattan, starting with sharing another fine meal at Becco.

Start spreading the news. Closing to a standing ovation, I now sing a wildly enthusiastic and totally out-of-tune rendition of "New York, New York." Eat your heart out, Frankie.

You Say Potluck, I Say Buffet

To Bradley, "dim sum"
is Chinese for all-you-can-eat.

The Cook

I hate potluck. There I've said it. There's no going back now. I hate going to and cooking for potluck. And I hate hosting potluck. But they are a fact of life, as sure as death or taxes. You can't escape potluck.

I have no problem with pot or with luck, but not when we're talking about food. Can you imagine going to a restaurant and the waiter says, "Tonight's dinner is potluck. Good luck with your meal."

When I go to a party I want to be fed; I want to be there without any obligations. Bringing a bottle of wine is certainly easy enough. Cooking part of a meal is work. And it is work that I do, not work that Mark does. He just goes, eats, and has a good time.

I have to cook, pack up whatever I've made, make sure it is hot enough, and make sure that I take my platter/bowl/whatever back with me. And, of course, clean up the mess I make when I cook. (Cleaning up is the worst part of cooking. At least for me.)

Giving a potluck party is almost worse. My inner control freak tries to take over and tell the guests what to make and bring. It is a losing situation. Sure, if I'm making a ham or other pork dish, your bean salad will be great. But maybe not so great with my cassoulet.

Living here in Mexico, I have an additional worry. Did you adequately disinfect those vegetables you brought? Are you careless with your food preparation? I don't want people thinking they got sick from something I cooked, when it was something someone else cooked.

It is always about blame and saving face.

Of course, I don't hate all potlucks. Just the dinner type ones. You know the kind. You get an invitation to a dinner party, accept and then before you know it, the hostess is asking you to bring the vegetable, or the dessert, or appetizers. I thought she was inviting me to dinner. No, she was inviting me to the main course!

Some potlucks are fun. Super bowl parties should always be potlucks. Who cares what is on the table as long as there is enough to drink? Spur of the moment, family-type dinners can also be potlucks. It is the sharing that is important.

As you might imagine, Thanksgiving is my favorite holiday. And, of course, Thanksgiving is the mother of all potlucks. One cook cannot—or should not—do all the cooking. However, I don't really consider Thanksgiving a potluck event. It is too structured and traditional. After all, no one brings a tuna casserole to Thanksgiving. At least, not to mine.

In Portland, Mark and I belonged to a gourmet dinner group. Each member brought a specific dish, according to a specific cuisine. This was not a potluck. It was planned and had structure, a purpose.

The absolute worst potlucks are company ones. All the women work hard at making something good, if not great, and the guys bring chips. Or bread. Or have their wife make something. Everyone gets together and eats and sure enough the men disappear before the clean-up.

I stopped going to company potlucks. Just like that: I stopped. Nobody missed me, which might say more about me than about potlucks.

As long as I'm on this subject, I have to say that I also hate buffets. It should not come as a surprise, after all, a potluck is just the home version of a restaurant buffet. Buffets are breeding grounds for a myriad of germs, if not really bad food that sits for hours in lukewarm steam trays. When I go to eat, I want to eat Italian food, or Chinese food, or good old American food (whatever that is). I don't want an unintentional array of fusion food that is not representational of any one cuisine. And I want to be waited on, not go from station to station like a beggar at the feast.

And now, a new look at Potlucks. It is interesting that as we—or maybe just me—age, we change our views. Yes, I hate potlucks. I still hate potlucks. But I am beginning, ever so slowly, to learn how to live with, if not love, potlucks.

What changed my mind? Age, money, community.

The older I get, the less energy I have to make a meal for large numbers of people. Gone now are the days of parties of 35, 75, even 100 people, with me doing all the cooking. I have come to the realization that I can't do it all. This has not been an easy realization. I hate the thought that I can't do what I used to do at 40, 50, or even 60. This is tough to say out loud.

Money. Yes, money. The root of all evil that we so like to create, hoard, spend, and divest. We all like—love—money. The thought of it; the smell of it; the comfort of it. When I was younger, money meant little to me. Oh, yes, at 22 I felt that if I made $10,000, all my problems would disappear. At 50, I thought I would work forever. I loved working and couldn't think of why I would ever stop. Slow—not fast—forward to 58 and I retired.

Money still means little to me. Health and community mean more than money. Can you really replace community with money? Don't think so.

Reality does set in and you realize that community does have a cost. That party costs more than your budget, but you really want to see that community. The only way to accomplish both is to share the costs by hosting a potluck.

Sigh.

I am willing to put aside my prejudices about potlucks for the sense of community that is more important to me.

There you have it. A change for probably the better, although I still hate potlucks!

Potlucks are a fact of life and we need to be prepared when asked to one. My potluck rules are few, but trustworthy.

Here are my rules for going to a potluck:

- Keep it simple. This is not a gourmet competition. You don't need to out-do anyone.

- Everyone loves deviled eggs. You can make them in advance and it doesn't matter if someone else makes them. They will all disappear.
- Try not to make something that needs to be reheated. You've worked enough by bringing something to the party, don't work AT the party. Learn to love room temperature food.
- Never sign up for the vegetable dish. Rarely does anyone eat it and it just sits there. Then you have to cart it back home.
- Do sign up for the green salad. Even if nobody actually eats it, everyone always takes some.

Rules for hosting a potluck:
- Why are you hosting a potluck? Get yourself out of this.
- If you have to host a potluck, give people categories of foods to bring. For example, the vegetable, the appetizers, the dessert, etc.
- Even better, print out a couple of recipes for each category and send to the participants. This won't make you popular, but it will make for a nice dinner and less stress for your inner control freak.
- Give up! Let the dishes fall where they may. Make it a free for all and hope for the best.

Potlucks are obviously here to stay and, in the end, I've learned to live with them. After all, it is the sharing of the food that really matters, not what we eat.

The Eater

In retrospect, it seems I grew up with family potlucks and grew fat with restaurant buffets. A major distinction between a potluck and a buffet, in my opinion, is that you're required to bring a dish to a potluck, whereas for a buffet all you need to bring is your empty stomach and stretch-waist pants.

As a kid, my family enjoyed hosting dinner parties. We almost always had someone staying for dinner, even during the school week. And we often hosted Thanksgiving for the extended family, which usually turned out to be a form of potluck. My mother would provide the traditional turkey, gravy, and stuffing, while other family members would agree to bring dishes to complement the entree.

It was natural for my mom to want to entertain. Her parents, my maternal grandparents, owned a small ranch in St. Helena, California, with almost 30 acres of land. Since their children and grandchildren were all within a two-hour's drive away, they entertained a lot of family and friends. My grandmother kept a large, white table cloth. When someone would join them for dinner for the first time, she would have them scrawl their name on the table cloth. Later, she'd embroider the name in a colorful thread, giving the family a memorable food-related record of visitors. Mostly, I think back fondly on those family potlucks.

Work potlucks, however, were a different story. At one job where I worked, a male manager was known within the company to be the first person to always sign up to bring a dish to a potluck. And that's because he always signed up to bring bread. No dish, no cooking involved. I understood his reasoning. Fortunately, I had a secret weapon: Arlene. I'd sign up to bring a dish and she'd make it. Before you complain about culinary appropriation, I should mention that I always gave Arlene full credit for making whatever food I contributed.

Then there are the mystery potlucks, ones you end up going to but should have known better. During our first time living in Mexico, a friend invited us to tag along with her to a potluck. She pitched it to us as a gathering with food for new arrivals in town, offering us a good chance to meet more people. The food was delivered by a malfunctioning time machine, because we were served a lot of the oldies but certainly not many of the goodies: cheese log, tuna casserole, olive-stuffed celery, unidentifiable canapes, something or someone encased in gelatin, and several bags of store-bought chips. To add insult to injured appetite, the host asked for donations to help pay for the event.

Potlucks. The mind boggles, the stomach turns. Which is why I shall now turn my attention to buffets: the mind still boggling, the stomach still turning.

Don't get me wrong. I willingly and happily walked both sides of a buffet line for many years. That is, until I met Arlene and she shared her apocalyptic vision of buffet dining: food sitting for hours; bacteria lurking in trays; people touching the food, and so on. Rather than dwell on that dark path, I'd like to say a few positive things about buffets.

A buffet meal can make the most sense in some cases. Although Arlene does not like buffets, she loves *dim sum*, which is a movable buffet feast that, unlike most buffets, doesn't sit out exposed to everyone and everything. The food moves quickly from the kitchen to a covered dome—at least that's the concept.

Now I want to talk about that singular anomaly and enduring monument to the sin of Gluttony: the all you can eat buffet. Pre-Arlene, I could be seen frequenting such buffets on a regular basis. At the time, I considered turning pro eater but the competition was too stiff. Competing with the likes of Joey Chestnut? Come on. Those guys were way out of my league.

Still, I took buffet dining seriously and always followed a process, which I am currently documenting. Here is an excerpt from the introduction to my planned book *An Epicurean's Field Guide to Navigating the All You Can Eat Buffet* (Now with scratch & sniff photos!):

> The savvy buffet eater is patient and plays the long game. The first thing he or she does, upon entering a buffet room, is to walk around the table

and study the layout, paying particular attention to where the higher-priced, more desirable foods are located—meats, seafood, poultry—what the pros call proteins. The eater abides by three rules: avoid filling side dishes, such as pasta and other starches; leave buried utensils buried; and above all, never touch the sneeze guard.

Much like casinos dealing multiple decks of blackjack from a shoe, restaurants stack the cost-factor in their favor by only putting out small plates. But I am not so easily fooled. Besides, I have two hands, each capable of holding a plate. During my reconnaissance, I might notice a middle-aged man filling his plate with cheap starches or limp salads. I would shake my head sadly and mumble to myself: Amateur. When it comes to an all-you-can-eat buffet, I know what I am doing—I have a plan.

Or at least, I have a theory. In practice, this is how it often unfolds. I am on my way to the carving section, but several eaters are already in line. Clearly, my plan is no longer a secret. I scan the rest of my buffet options, and out of the corner of my eye, I spot a bin of macaroni and cheese; on such fleeting moments a noble cause is lost. Pasta is my kryptonite, you see. Powerless, I fill up my plate with pasta—mac and cheese, lasagna, ravioli, spaghetti with tiny meatballs so small they could be capers. I sit and eat, waiting for the carving line to shorten. By the time I am finished with my pastapalooza, I am nearly full and no longer interested in any proteins. Carbs—the Eighth Deadly Sin. Instead, I graze the desserts and pick a few. As I prepare to leave, I notice nobody is in the carving line and I dash over.

Those days for me are long gone. At the time, I didn't know any better.

In thinking back over my life, I am amazed I have lived this long. As a kid, I was oral-fixated, or so I am told, and ate everything from crayons to school paste, possibly even dirt, according to at least one rumor. Fortunately, one taste of any of those questionable food items was usually enough, and I never tried it again. At least not often. A few times, perhaps, to get a second or third opinion.

But a buffet was an entirely new experience. So many choices, such small plates. What's an eater to do?

Breakfast is Now Being Served

You have to be pretty aggressive
these days if you want a refill
on your coffee.

The Cook

This is a topic that Mark likes. Me? I am not a breakfast person.

I come from a family of non-breakfast eaters. My mother NEVER got up early enough—she worked nights as a waitress—to make me breakfast before school. My father got up very early and left before I was up and about. He had coffee and some sort of pastry before he went to work. Sometimes he met some friends at a coffee shop before work.

On Sundays, my father would buy an assortment of fish—white fish, lox—for breakfast, along with baked goods. Everyone, except me, loved eating cake or Danish or whatever for breakfast. I've never liked cake for breakfast.

Most mornings these days, I eat a piece of toast, with a bit of butter, maybe some cheese. Or an English muffin. If I am feeling virtuous, I'll slather peanut butter on my toast. Or avocado.

That's it. That's breakfast to me six days a week. On the seventh day, I cook.

Bacon and eggs are always a sure winner. Lately, I've been cooking my eggs in the bacon grease. Decadent, I know. But they do taste great.

Usually, though, I make a frittata. The great thing about a frittata—and there are tons of great things about a frittata—is that it allows me to use up bits and pieces of leftovers. I always seem to have bits and pieces of stuff in the refrigerator. Pieces of steak or pork. Cooked vegetables. End pieces of cheese. I use it all in my frittata. And the best thing is that there is usually some of the frittata leftover that Mark can eat it during the week. The leftover left over, so to speak.

I also like to cook hash. I make corned beef hash, of course. But also hash with leftover salmon, beef, or even pork. I may try lamb hash soon since we are getting great lamb here now.

I have to say the best corned beef hash I've had is a corned beef hash benedict. The hollandaise sauce really added a great dimension to the dish. I haven't tried to make it yet. It is difficult to find corned beef here in the middle of Mexico. And I haven't yet mastered hollandaise. It is on my to-do list.

I also have to say I make a great huevos rancheros. I have managed to streamline the recipe so that it is not as daunting. I buy jarred salsa—I love the Herdez brand. It is sold everywhere now, even in the States. The red salsa *casera* is milder than the green. You decide. Toast tortillas in a dry pan. Set aside. Heat the salsa in a large skillet, then add a can of drained and rinsed black beans. Cook until warm. (You can add a bit of water if it gets too dry.)

Additionally, you can cook the eggs any way you want. Place the bean/salsa mixture on top of the tortillas, add the egg(s), then a bit of cheese, maybe an avocado and some sour cream.

There you have it.

Baked eggs. I love baked eggs. You do any combination and it always comes out great. Greens on the bottom, some bacon or other meat or salmon (great for leftover salmon). Some heavy cream, then the eggs. Of course, Sunday breakfast should be decadent. When I have leftover salmon, I often make salmon cakes. If I have some salmon cakes leftover, I heat them up and put an egg on it. Voila! A fancy breakfast made with leftovers.

To me, breakfast is a feast of leftovers. Just don't tell Mark.

The Eater

I'm an early morning person. I always have been an early-bird type, I guess. No matter how late I stay up or get home the night before, I am physically unable to remain in bed until noon. In fact, I can't recall when or if I ever slept in as late as 10 A.M., other than when I had the flu. Even in retirement, I rise before the crack of dawn. It's a curse.

Or, maybe, it's a blessing. By getting up early, I have more time left in the day to accomplish many wonderful things, such as create a new support group (*Singles with Shingles*) or write my latest how-to book (*Yodeling Under Water for Fun and Profit*) or take out the trash. I'm normally awake and out of bed by six in the morning; some days, I'm a slug and sleep in until seven. All of which means, breakfast ranks high on my list of daily accomplishments.

One time, when my sister and I, as young kids, spent the night at a friend's house, the friend's mother asked what we wanted for breakfast. We both said "Eggs on toast." Naturally, the woman made us a couple of eggs and dropped them on top of a piece of toast. We were disappointed, if not aghast. The dish we knew by that name was an egg cooked in an opening in the middle of pan-fried bread. According to an online article published at MyRecipes.com, that particular dish has at least 66 different names, from toad-in-a-hole to gas house eggs, from Marty Wilson to Adam and Eve on a Raft. No wonder my friend's mother was confused. On the other hand, as an adult watching one of my all-time favorite movies, *Moonstruck,* I was thrilled to watch the Olympia Dukakis character make the same dish. In the movie, the breakfast dish was called *uova nel cestino,* or "eggs in a waste basket." One person's breakfast is another person's trash.

My point is when it comes to eating breakfast, I'm all-in and I leave nothing for the trash can. I can eat it any time of day and eat almost anything. At home, I make my own breakfast six days a week. On Sundays, Arlene makes a delicious frittata. And any meal with bacon is a keeper.

I suppose I developed my early morning habit early in life. Thinking back on it, I was a lucky kid, especially whenever I visited family in the San Francisco Bay area. My grandparents on my mother's side owned a ranch in St. Helena, the very heart of the wine country, and gave me, a suburbanite from Sacramento, a taste of country living; my father's parents lived on the first-level of an Edwardian-style two-story flat in Oakland, giving me a more urban experience. My father's parents even had a Murphy Bed, an ingenious invention to a young mind.

My maternal grandfather worked at the Mare Island Naval Yard in Vallejo, an hour's drive from the ranch. He was a welder and one of the first to do underwater welding. Before driving in to work, he'd get up at dawn and take care of the animals. He was a true rancher, not a wine grower, and reminded me of the actor Ward Bond. Sometimes, I'd sit with him during those early mornings and join him for breakfast. He would always put a splash of coffee in his bowl of shredded wheat, a habit I still follow today.

My paternal grandfather in Oakland would rise before anyone else in the flat. I would join him in the kitchen with the wood stove, and he would make us bacon and eggs. The eggs would be crispy from the bacon grease. We would be done with breakfast and out the door before the others knew we were gone. I suspect their plan was to get me out of the house and keep me out until much later in the day. My grandfather was a supervisor for Western Pacific Railroad and never owned a car, which meant he was a walker. We walked through Oakland, all day long, and walking in a city is another habit I enjoy to this day.

When Arlene and I took my parents on a Holland American cruise through Alaska's Inside Passage, we assumed we'd be doing more eating than usual. After all, cruising is just another word for nothing left to do but overeat. According to what I had read—and later experienced—the average person gains one to two pounds for each day of cruising. We were on a seven-day cruise, so our bottom floor (no pun intended) was a gain of seven pounds. And we did our best to rise from that floor, when possible, every chance we got.

For example, we had made reservations for an off-ship excursion for our stay in Skagway. One night at our assigned dinner table, we told the others about the excursion, scheduled for the following morning. The excursion was called something like "Wilderness Glacier Outdoor Adventure Yadda Yadda Yadda," and it involved flying to a small strip of land, busing as far in as they could take us, walking a half-mile through the wilderness, reaching canoes, paddling up a river and onto a glacial lake, where we would spend time exploring the lake, after which, we were to be treated to a salmon bake on the lake's shore. The discussion at our table eventually turned to the possibility of running into bear. That's when some wag at the table told the old joke about two guys being chased by a bear. One guy stops to put on his tennis shoes. His friend tells him better shoes won't help: you can't outrun a bear. The other guy replies, "I don't have to outrun the bear. I only have to outrun you."

Two groups of us arrived at the small airport in the morning and boarded two small planes. We were flown to a strip of land, where, as promised, we boarded a bus that took us as far as the road would allow. We left the bus to walk the rest of the way but were told to be careful, because of reported bear activity. The guides wanted us to stay close together and make as much noise as we could during our hike to the river. At the river, we were assigned canoes, with each canoe headed by a staff member. The lake was incredibly pristine, with the kind of shocking blue one only sees on Nature shows with a high-resolution TV set. While on the lake, the weather changed and it began to rain. The staff person chatted on a walkie-talkie for a few minutes and then told us we were returning to shore.

A storm was coming in and we all had to leave. No salmon bake. Sorry, folks. Better luck next time. Instead, they told us to make us much noise as we could and run as fast as we could to get to the bus. If we didn't take off in time, we would be forced to spend the night in a nearby cabin and wait until the weather improved. Apparently, our pilots were not able to fly using instruments because of surrounding mineral deposits; they needed to be able to see. Message received, loud and clear.

Arlene ran faster than I'd seen her run in a long time. She reminded me she'd had lox and bagels for breakfast every morning. To a bear, she would make a tasty snack. She told me later that after she passed an 85-year-old woman, leaving the older woman in her wake, she relaxed her pace a bit. She had finally outrun somebody and was no longer the obvious buffet choice. We all made it back to the plane together and our planes lifted off just as the menacing dark clouds closed in. We landed safely in Skagway and were bused back to the ship, where Arlene and I raced up the gang plank, hoping to reach the dining room before it closed. And we almost made it, too, missing lunch service by mere minutes. We pressed our faces to the glass of the dining room door, hoping to find a waiter to let us in. My parents were sitting inside finishing their lunch, saw us, and waved. We must have looked pathetic, like hungry street urchins in an O. Henry short story, peering in at a fancy Manhattan restaurant and watching all the swells commit gluttony. But truth be told, we were not hungry, and the last thing we needed, the absolute last thing, was another meal.

Still, as an eater I had a reputation to uphold. I remembered they were serving meals on the Lido Deck and made my way there lickety-split. Score! They were still serving breakfast.

Five Foods in Hell

That's not soup.
That's simmering potpourri.

The Cook

Some cooks have the reputation of eating everything, including all parts of the animal. That kind of cook is not me. I am fussy. I have always been a fussy eater. As a child, I ate little meat, a few vegetables (always canned!), and salad. I had a small appetite. One thing I always ate was bread—any kind of bread—and butter.

As I grew older, I expanded my diet. I ate fish, a bit more of meat, and lots of salad. My mother worked in a steak-house and I always ordered my NY Steak well-done. Just to drive her crazy. Which it did. As I entered my twenties, I modified well-done to medium, making my mother much happier.

I went through a phase of eating odd things, like kidneys. That phase didn't last long.

So, here I am. What the hell will I be forced to eat, or cook, in Hell?

When I was a child, the food I would be forced to eat in Hell would be gefilte fish, specifically my grandmother's gefilte fish. Actually, as a child, anything my grandmother made would be a food that I would be forced to eat. I have since learned how to cook a great gefilte fish using salmon. It has the taste of old-fashioned gefilte fish without the slime.

As a young adult, I have to say that Chinese food would fit the bill of foods in Hell. Not that I didn't enjoy some Chinese food, but that my first husband wanted to eat only Chinese food. I felt like I was in Hell most of the time. We lived in New York where the best Chinese food exists—at least I think so. But New York also has the best Italian and French food in the nation. Hell to me at that time was having to ALWAYS eat Chinese food.

I used to hate peanut butter. But that has passed. I used to hate coconut. But can tolerate it now.

Where am I now? If I go to Hell, what will I be forced to eat or cook?

Shrimp. I know EVERYONE eats shrimp. People who hate fish eat shrimp. I can eat one, maybe two, before stopping. I don't know why I don't like it. I'll eat scallops, any kind of fish, even raw oysters. But not shrimp. I wasn't always like this. At parties, I used to gobble up stuffed shrimp. Now, I turn my back on any kind of shrimp dish. I make a great shrimp scampi, for example, but refuse to eat it.

Okra. Can't get past the slime factor. Enough said. Okra is an acquired taste that I don't have the time to acquire. Or learn how to cook. This may change but I doubt it.

Nopales. See above. Same problem, same outcome.

Offal. Any of it and all of it. Well, except for liver, especially chicken liver. Is there anything better than chopped liver on a sandwich with onion and tomato? Or spread on a cracker? There is a Peruvian restaurant here in San Miguel that has sauteed chicken livers on their menu. What a treat!

And tongue. I grew up eating tongue. I never thought of it as, well, tongue. I just thought that's what it was called, not what it was, or is. I haven't eaten tongue in many years, but would be okay with it in a sandwich. With a little mustard. On good rye bread.

But I can't think of cooking or eating other offal, such as snouts, heads, eyes, trotters, or feet. And we won't even go into anus (pun intended). Or out of it for that matter. Intestines, kidney, heart, lungs are also off my list to eat or cook.

Milk. I haven't had a glass of milk in almost 70 years. Yes, you read that right. When my sister was born—I was almost three—I told my mother that I was a big girl now and didn't need a bottle. She was thrilled until she realized that I really meant that I didn't want to drink milk. She put chocolate in milk (remember Bosco?) to get me to drink it. I had fits in kindergarten when the teacher made me drink milk out of the carton. I gag thinking about it now. At four I had my tonsils taken out—a rite of passage for those times—and the worst part of it was having them force-feed me milk. I think I am lactose intolerant. Or maybe I just hate milk.

Other People's Cooking. Okay, this is a bit of a reach but not too far of a reach. I hate eating food that some guy, who doesn't know how to cook, barbeques the hell out of a piece of meat or fish (usually salmon). The meat or fish is

already dead. You don't need to kill it twice. Or three times.
Give a man a barbeque and, all of a sudden, he becomes a
chef. I hate mayonnaise as a cooking ingredient. I've tried
cooking with it, slathering it on a piece of fish. I even tried
it on a grilled cheese sandwich. Ugh. It just doesn't work
for me. I used to be totally mayonnaise intolerant, but have
decided it is okay mixed with tuna fish. Or mixed with sriracha for a chicken taco.

Bottled Salad Dressings. I also hate store-bought
salad dressings. It takes so little to make a decent one. All
you need is a decent olive oil and vinegar. If you are a bit
more ambitious, here's a "secret" recipe for blue cheese
dressing that was created by the steakhouse restaurant
where my mother worked.

*Roquefort Blue Cheese Dressing: Lenny's Res-
taurant*
- Crumbled Roquefort blue cheese—
  chunky
- Worcestershire sauce
- A garlic clove, minced
- Mayonnaise
- Mix all ingredients together. If too
  thick, add a little water.

I know. Specific amounts are not listed, except for the
one garlic clove. You'll have to taste your way through this
recipe to make it work.

The Eater

What five foods will I be force-fed in Hell? Wait a minute. Are you telling me the many Saturdays I spent saying Confession to a priest as a kid didn't pay off as advertised, and I'm going to the bad place after all? No way. I want a refund!

With no refund available, I see myself creeping along a narrow rocky path, purple haze swirling around me, sinister ravens nipping at my neck. Encouraged to move forward by a pitchfork methodically jabbing my bare backside to the tune of "In-A-Gadda-Da-Vida" (the long version), I approach the entrance to a cave and notice a sign above its opening. I chuckle to myself, as I read it. An old hand-painted Abandon All Hope sign has been updated with a new message. The new corporate-looking sign employs a customized sans-serif font (ahem, Hellvetica) and displays this message:

Welcome to Hell®.
The original inventor of the Weeping & Gnashing
of Teeth™ torture method.
Do not be fooled by cheap imitations.

At the entrance to the pit that is bottomless, I see another sign, this one hand-drawn with a thick Sharpie pen: "Our Promise to You, Ye Damned Souls. We will do all we can to make your stay with us in Eternity as miserable as we can make it. That's a promise!"

Attesting to the sign's commitment, a mix of signed names appears under it, including Satan, Lucifer, Devil, Beelzebub, Baal the Prince, Son of Perdition, Mammon, Gorgo, Mephistopheles, Old Scratch, and The Evil One, as well as several unreadable names obviously scrawled and scratched by those with hoof-like appendages instead of hands.

This Welcome to Hell sign was a result of an offsite team-building workshop led by a marketing consulting firm and attended by all those signing, in a show of bonded support. One imagines, it must have been quite the workshop, especially since so many of their expensed items are still under dispute by Accounts Payable.

All right, enough with the prologue. It's time I roll up my sleeves and discuss how those hellcats can make my eternity miserable through food. Quite frankly, I think it will be challenging for them, because as an eater, I'm known to eat just about anything put on my plate or someone else's plate. Still, I have boundaries, low as they might be.

For example, I do not believe in the 5-second rule; if it's on the ground, it's dog food. Unlike Andrew Zimmern, you won't catch me eating Bamboo Rat, on or off a stick, or the placenta of any mammal. And I don't even want to talk about that guy on TV who makes a living trying to eat more than his body weight in food. I'm an eater, not a glutton.

That said, I have a high acceptance rate for foods others might find repulsive or inedible, including cilantro, mushrooms, beets, broccoli, olives, black licorice, and so on. I also find disgusting some foods others adore. For instance, I don't like caviar and I may be in a small minority holding that opinion. For me, caviar is too close to salmon eggs, which I used in my younger years as bait when fishing for trout. Eating caviar on a cracker would be the same to me as eating hellgrammites on crostini, and if you've ever seen a hellgrammite, you know how unappetizing that makes the crostini.

So, Maestro, cue the music. Without further qualification, here are the five foods I will most likely be forced to eat in the afterlife, against my will, and as a form of a richly-deserved punishment.

Creamed Corn. I've had an aversion to creamed corn since I was a child. Unlike the plastic fake-vomit you could buy at a Gag Shop, this food item is too close to the real thing in texture and appearance to enable me to eat it. Don't get me wrong. I like corn-on-the-cob and other forms of corn, from chowders to popcorn. I'm just not a big fan of upchucked food. Lips that have touched cream corn shall never touch mine.

Eggplant. Consider the unharvested eggplant, which is both sleek and beautiful. Now, think about what's inside. Unfortunately, I can't stand the taste of eggplant, and it's not just its well-known bitterness. I like plenty of bitter things: Brussels sprouts, Arugula, Chocolate, Satire. There is something bordering on the inedible for me with eggplant. I realize I'm part of a minority report on the vegetable, especially since Arlene and so many others find it delicious. For me, eggplant comes under the *no más* category.

Herring. I would not be surprised to learn that pickled herring is Arlene's favorite food. She loves it, as many people do. A friend of ours from Sweden would host an annual party where he shared an assortment of herring, along with mustards for dipping and plenty of akvavit to wash it down. My paternal grandmother was Swedish but I'll stick to meatballs (thank you, IKEA) and baked salmon. You can hold that jar of pickled herring, in the immortal words of Jack Nicholson, between your knees.

Liver. When I was on the high school wrestling team and on a strict diet, the only protein I ate was liver, because of its reported high-iron content. Since those days, I can't stand the taste, sight, or smell of liver--even with fava beans and a nice Chianti. Granted, I can still eat *pâté*, but an entire slab of pan-fried liver has me running in the other direction.

Raw Oysters. I like smoked oysters, but who doesn't? You can put a cowboy boot through the smoking process and it becomes edible. Raw oysters are another matter. They're disgusting. I imagine on some coastal town in the world there's a plaque in honor of the first human to eat a raw oyster. The poor guy must have been desperate, having already consumed all the seaweed and lichen within reach and lacking the eye-hand coordination required to catch fish. In a last-ditch effort to stave off hunger, he cracked open an oyster, slurped it down, and called it good. I call it slimy.

Okay, so that's what my disagreeable hosts will serve me as food. If I needed to list an unappealing food as an alternate, it would be cottage cheese. All of which begs the question, what will I drink? That's easy. Whatever they call that prep drink you must take before getting a colonoscopy. In my opinion, that prep drink is Hell's signature cocktail. No contest.

Five Foods in Heaven

How's the monkfish today?

The Cook

Truth be told, my vision of Heaven is that I can and do eat everything, even those things I would have to eat in Hell. In Heaven, calories don't count and there is no such thing as high cholesterol or high blood pressure.

All food is good.

The bigger question is whether I would cook. In Heaven, food would always be available and would always be good, fantastic even. My vision is that I would think of a dish—grilled lamb chops, let's say—and it would appear. Ready to eat and delicious.

So why would I cook? Granted, cooking is a creative outlet for me but do I really need to cook if I am in Heaven and can do or be anything I want to be. I could paint, write, play the piano, dance. I am not sure that I would cook.

Been there, done that.

I would love to garden; I'm sure everything in Heaven grows beautifully. I would grow vegetables and herbs and some flowers to add color. I guess I would have to cook to use the bounty from my garden. Even in Heaven, you don't want to waste anything.

I'm getting hungry. So here, for what it is worth, are the five foods I would cook in Heaven.

Pesto. I love Pesto and in Heaven I would have the time and the energy to try new versions. I usually make pesto with basil, garlic, parmesan cheese, and pine nuts. Sometimes I go crazy with myself and use walnuts instead of pine nuts. Good, but not very adventuresome. In Heaven, I could make pesto with fennel fronds, or mustard greens, or even carrot or radish greens.

Ratatouille. Ratatouille is one of my all-time favorite dishes. Eggplant, zucchini, yellow peppers all swimming with cherry tomatoes. What could be better? I love it on an English Muffin, a bit of cheese sprinkled on the top and then microwaved. Or wrapped in a tortilla. I can eat ratatouille every day for lunch and never tire of it.

Herring. I don't cook herring. I just eat it. Enough said. I guess in Heaven, I could eat it in cream sauce, or rolled up with cucumber or something inside. Who knows? In Heaven, I could become the Herring Queen, finding new and more delicious ways to eat it.

Bread. A day without bread is like a day without sunshine. Bread just makes everything better. I haven't baked bread in many, many years. During the pandemic, when many people were making loaf after loaf of sourdough bread, I was making chicken pot pies. (We won't even go there!) In Heaven, I am sure that I would renew my love of baking bread. Long baguettes, rye bread, heavy, dark pumpernickel. Quick breads and slow breads. Zucchini bread, banana bread, Irish soda bread. I would make them all. And then eat them all.

Cheese. Since I am in Heaven and don't have to worry about cholesterol or lactose intolerance, I could make and eat cheese to my heart's content. I would learn how to make goat cheeses, all kinds. I would make mascarpone and bur-rata and mozzarella. I might even have some goats to make all this easier. Cheeses that go well with my breads.

Food in Heaven is, well, heavenly. For now, I'll stick to earthly delights.

The Eater

Back in The Pleistocene, I attended Catholic School and ever since I've been fascinated with views of the afterlife as depicted in popular culture. For example, we know what can happen to us if we say "Beetlejuice" three times. But what happens if Beetlejuice says your name three times? Didn't think of that one, did you?

Perspectives on the afterlife can be as diverse as life itself. For instance, in the dark comedy *Steambath*, a play by Bruce Jay Friedman, the newly departed wait for what's coming next in a public steam bath, where God is a Puerto Rican janitor. "An Extract from Captain Stormfield's Visit to Heaven" is a short story by Mark Twain that remains one of my all-time favorites: people whose talent went unrecognized on earth are duly honored in the afterlife by the likes of Homer, Shakespeare, and Buddha; a bittersweet piece of satire about celebrity status.

More recently, the TV show *The Good Place*, took place in the afterlife. It was preceded several years earlier by the movie *Defending Your Life*, which took place not in Heaven but in a celestial city on the way there. While in this way-station of a city, the story's protagonist, played by Albert Brooks, is shown video clips from his life on earth; he has to defend his actions to qualify for entry through the pearly gates.

Did the Albert Brooks character get in? You'll have to watch the movie to find out. I'm not interested in talking about the success or failure of his litigation. That said, I really want to talk about how that movie covered the topic of food. Although it may not have been the precise definition or location of Heaven, it was Heaven for an eater, such as myself. In *Defending Your Life*, you could eat or drink anything and not have to pay for any of it—or, best of all, gain any weight. If I somehow slip through the cracks and find myself in the good place, here are five foods or meals that will be waiting for me.

A **Bone-in Ribeye Steak**, with plenty of marbling, started in the oven and finished on the grill for that seared, smokey flavor, which would also enhance the "house" dry rub, a mixture of cracked black pepper, paprika, garlic powder, cayenne pepper, crushed red pepper, and, of course, plenty of kosher salt. This would be served with a baked potato, smothered in butter and sour cream, and honey garlic green beans. If they're out of ribeye, I will happily settle for prime rib.

Fresh Dungeness crab from the Pacific Northwest, complemented by a sourdough baguette and a fresh spring salad mix with a light vinaigrette topped with blue cheese crumbles. An acceptable substitute would be using the same sweet crab in a Cioppino dish, along with prawns, clams, and a meaty white fish such as ling cod. If I could sneak in scallops, I would. Perhaps as a side, I could get pan-seared scallops, with deep-fried shallots on top, and all drizzled with a light splash of maple syrup.

Stuck for eternity? Then I must be served a plate of **Southern Fried Chicken**, and from everything I've read the go-to place for the best fried chicken is Willie Mae's Scotch House in New Orleans. I've been to the Big Easy but missed out on Willie Mae's. Because this time I'll be in the afterlife and won't be able to get to New Orleans easily, I'll place a special to-go order with Uber for Willie Mae's fried chicken (Food Network and the Travel Channel both claim it's the best in America). I'll also order a full set of traditional accompaniments, such as macaroni and cheese, butterbeans, and mashed potatoes with gravy, along with a side of red beans and rice.

I can't and won't spend eternity without Asian food. The challenge is I like so much of it, even though I've never mastered the art of using chop sticks, what Bill Bryson calls "knitting needles." It's very difficult to limit myself to one Asian dish. From Thai to Vietnamese, Japanese to Chinese, not to mention Korean, I can eat Asian food every day of the week. Which begs the question: Do they even have days in Heaven?

Rather than go upscale or esoteric, I'm going to choose **Beef Chow Fun** from an old hole-in-the-wall restaurant in San Francisco's Chinatown called "Sam Woo." The restaurant is no longer in its original location, but, hey, this is my afterlife and I'll order what I want and from where I want. The egg noodles are wide, the beef is nicely spiced, the scallions are plentiful, and everything is served hot. Plus, it's all greasy. When the restaurant was in its original location, the food was delivered from the kitchen by way of a dumb waiter elevator and served by the legendary waiter Edsel Ford Fong, called the "world's rudest, worst, most insulting waiter."

The first time Arlene took me to Sam Woo Restaurant, I was enthralled. The place was tiny, and you walked through the kitchen to get upstairs to the dining room, which was full of eaters happily engaged in conversation and ingesting food. It was far noisier than the street traffic outside. Edsel Ford would sneak kisses from the women guests and ignore anyone who asked for silverware, including me. My concern is Mr. Fong ended up in the other place. Nonetheless, their Beef Chow Fun was unforgettable, and only he could serve it. With so much grease, the food sailed down my throat like a kid in summer on a Slip-n-Slide. The verdict? Delicious.

Of the many fantastic meals Arlene has made and I've eaten over the years, I'm barely able to narrow my choice to two options, let alone pick a single meal. The first is, of course, her **spaghetti carbonara**, which I could easily die for or from. The second would be her **rack of lamb** served with her special scalloped potatoes. Yummy in both cases. I'm not sure which one to choose, so I'll have to come back later to decide, perhaps by flipping a coin. After all, I'll be in the afterlife with plenty of time on my hands. Wait! Stop the presses. I almost forgot Arlene's delicious *coq au vin* and her equally yummy *cassoulet* and her lighter-than-air lamb meatball soup. Hmm. This could take a while.

Finally, I've reached the dessert course. There's no question which dessert I want to be served in Heaven: my mom's **cheesecake**. Simply put, it was creamy, rich, and delicious, nestled in a crust with the perfect texture. Family and friends alike always asked my mom to make cheesecake whenever we had a social gathering. When, as a kid, I heard adults talk about her cheesecake, I was confused. The thought of a piece of American cheese resting on top of a slice of sugary chocolate cake didn't thrill me. Then, again, I was unclear on the concept of cheesecake, to say the least, as well as so much more in life. Once I tasted my mother's cheesecake, I understood why so many people loved it. She didn't smother the dessert with berries or chocolate syrup. Her cheesecake was unadulterated and stood alone. It still does.

I know it might seem odd to ask for specific meals in Heaven, a place where you can get anything to eat you want and as much of it. However, I like to think when I'm dining at one of Heaven's gazillion restaurants, no matter which one, the waiter will ask me if I want to hear tonight's specials. I would say yes, and the waiter would proceed to tell me about all my favorite dishes, including the five I cited above, making me feel, uh, how shall I put this, it would make me feel very special.

Let's face it, a man's appetite should exceed his menu, or what's a Heaven for?

How Much is that Veggie in the Window?

Oregon Mushroom Hunters

The Cook

Vegetables! Vegetables! Wherefore art thou?

One day at work, sitting in my cubicle, I overheard a conversation about hunting. The guy was on the phone and talking loudly about killing a deer and having to "dismantle" it so he could get it home.

I was sick over it and decided right then and there to become a vegetarian.

Mark was not happy.

I decided that as of January 1, I would no longer eat any meat or fish. I would be a total vegetarian. If Mark wanted to have meat or fish, he would have to make it himself or go out to eat. You can imagine how popular this was in our house.

And so, this life change began.

I cooked a variety of vegetarian dishes, most of which I have forgotten. I know I made lots of pasta, a casserole of vegetables with cheese. I can't remember what else.

In March 1988, *Babette's Feast* was released and we went to the movies to see it. Watching that movie was the end of my vegetarianism. On the way home, we bought steaks.

However, I have never lost my love of vegetables. Just last week, I had the most amazing dish of vegetables in mole. Outstanding. I can't wait to make it myself.

Mole is made with chicken stock, but could as easily be made with water or vegetable stock, making it a great vegetarian sauce. It has nuts, seeds, chocolate, and a vast array of other ingredients. Making mole takes a whole day or two and a team of cooks. Nowadays, I prefer to buy mole paste and reconstitute it with chicken stock. I use this on chicken enchiladas and now I'm going to try it with vegetables. Certainly not a true vegetarian meal. I guess you could call it flexitarian.

Whatever.

In Medford, Oregon, I had four fairly large raised garden beds, and I grew a variety of vegetables, along with herbs. We always had zucchini, eggplant (my favorite!), bell peppers, shishito peppers (another favorite) and tomatoes. Lots of tomatoes. Basically, I grew vegetables for my ratatouille, which I ate for lunch almost every day.

Ratatouille. I LOVE ratatouille. It has all my favorites: Eggplant, zucchini, peppers, onion, tomatoes, garlic. Sometimes I add a bit of ginger, some garbanzo beans.

Next to ratatouille—I just love writing that word—is pesto. I am growing an inordinate amount of basil here in Mexico. It is almost like a weed. Is basil a vegetable? Are herbs veggies? Who cares? Basil is just wonderful. And pesto is basil on steroids, at least as far as I'm concerned.

I have some Italian basil and some Mexican basil (whatever that is, but it smells like basil to me). I mix them to make my pesto, sometimes with walnuts and sometimes with pine nuts. Either way, it is great.

I love to make spaghetti with pesto. It is really just boiling water, cooking the pasta and then adding the pesto. What could be easier? Vegetarian and almost vegan.

I could become vegetarian again, I think, but never vegan. I'm not a big cheese eater, but I would have to forgo my beloved pesto.

I guess I would always have my ratatouille.

The Eater

As a cartoonist, I've paid a boatload of attention to gag cartoons in my time. Along with recalling meals consumed, I usually can recall cartoons admired from long ago, in a kingdom by the sea. A famous cartoon, for example, from the early days of *The New Yorker*, showed a child refusing to eat her vegetables. In the caption, the mother tells her daughter what's on her plate is broccoli. The unconvinced daughter fires back by telling her mother it's spinach and to hell with it. The cartoon was drawn by Carl Rose and captioned by E.B. White.

Unlike a former U.S. president who banned broccoli from the White House menu and from Air Force One, I happen to like the "b" word. I also like spinach. So, there. To hell with the vegetable haters.

I do have my boundaries, however. I believe slathering heavy sauces over something that happily grew outside in the bright sun and fresh air borders on the criminal. I prefer my vegetables with only slight alterations: fresh and not canned, cooked with butter or olive oil, grilled or roasted or steamed. In fact, I enjoy eating just about any vegetable, with the possible exception of eggplant. I know a large part of the dining world loves eggplant, including Arlene, but its tasty charms elude me. On the other hand, I respect how the vegetable looks in nature: deep purple and oblong, like some kind of custom-made exotic sports car kept in Elon Musk's garage.

I don't recall being overly fussy about eating vegetables as a kid. But later in life, I reacted to asparagus. One morning my urine had an odd smell. Back then, I was a member in good standing of the Hypochondriac's Club and told Arlene I needed to see a doctor. I was examined and a urine sample was taken. We sat outside the doctor's office waiting for the bad news. He popped his head out and asked if I had eaten any asparagus lately. Arlene and I nodded. He said that was the cause; I was suffering from what is known as asparagus pee. The numbers vary but studies indicate up to 50 percent of those who eat asparagus experience the smell. Ah, spring, when a young man's urine turns to sulfur.

It takes a lot for me to not eat the vegetables on my plate. And it doesn't matter if it is broccoli, brussels sprouts, cucumber, green beans, zucchini, carrots, cabbage, peppers, peas, or something that looked it just arrived from another planet or dimension. They are all welcome at my table. I am particularly fond of potatoes. Nothing complements a juicy steak like a baked russet potato, in my opinion, or fried chicken like mashed potatoes. French fries are a given; Arlene's potatoes *au gratin*, a treat. If offered the choice between pancakes or hash brown potatoes, mark me down for the spuds every time. True confession: one of my guilty pleasures is Tater Tots®, grated potatoes formed into the shape of small barrels and deep-fried. I know this violates my preference for unadulterated vegetables, but hey, life is full of exceptions.

Masala dosa is one of my favorite potato dishes. If we are dining at an East Indian restaurant and *masala dosa* is on the menu, we'll order it, because it is both delicious and a perfect dish for sharing. The outer shell is a thin, crepe-like bread; inside of this shell is a spicy mashed potato mix. To eat it, you break off the bread and use it to scoop and eat the potato filling. Now, that is, of course, a hungry layman's description and may not be how the dish is formally—or even correctly—described. The key takeaway is that the dish is all-vegetarian. No red meat, white chicken, or blue tuna inside of the crepe.

Which brings me to the topic of salads. I don't know how it brings me there, but here I am, so let's talk about salads for a moment.

Arlene and I may disagree on many food topics but we are in total agreement when it comes to salad dressing. We make our own vinaigrette and eschew those bottled salad dressings sold in stores. It is so easy to make I don't know why anyone would settle for pre-packaged, bottled dressings: 3 parts olive oil and 1 part vinegar, shaken not stirred, or stirred not shaken, and poured. Sometimes we might add a drop of something spicy or flavorful. We usually add blue cheese crumbles to the top of the dressed salad.

Making a basic dinner salad is one of the kitchen skills I am allowed to perform; I feel like a teenager who is not allowed anywhere near the kitchen at home but who gets to wear a paper hat and make salads as a *sous-chef* at a local fast-food joint after school. In addition to the usual lettuce mix, chopped scallions, radish, and mushrooms, I like to add croutons, walnuts, or garbanzo beans, when available. Arlene makes a delicious caprese salad, using basil from our own garden, and will serve it as a first-course when entertaining guests for dinner. Occasionally, we'll make an entrée salad together for our main meal. One of our favorite salads is what we generically call a Mexican salad: plenty of lettuce, thinly-sliced red onions, radish, grated cheese (Monterey Jack preferred), black beans, and tortilla chips. We dress it with a vinaigrette and serve grilled tortillas on the side.

One New Year's Eve, Arlene and I made a resolution to become vegetarians during the coming year. I lasted all of two-weeks, an agonizing fortnight. Much to her strong-willed credit, Arlene survived nearly six months as a vegetarian. That is, until she ran into a tantalizing buzzsaw known as the movie *Babette's Feast*. She later accused me of treachery, but we both willingly went to see the movie at a local theater—I didn't force her. If you are unaware of the film, and you love an honest story about what it means to be a part of humanity, see it. *Babette's Feast* is about spirituality, friendship, and yes, the making of a mouthwatering multi-course meal. On our way home that evening, we stopped by a grocery store, loaded up on food, and made our own feast, heavy on the proteins and light on the other stuff. Tofu was not being served.

Frankly, I still have a hard time considering tofu a protein. To me, eating tofu is like chewing on a memory foam pillow.

It's Always Happy Hour Somewhere

I never buy a wine that
costs less than a corkscrew.

The Cook

I love Happy Hour. What's not to love? At the end of the day, you sit down with your loved one, perhaps a friend or two, have a drink (martinis!) and a snack or two.

Of course, the real trick is not to eat, or drink, too much and spoil dinner. Most of the time, we're controlled and just have one drink and a small treat. But sometimes we go all the way and eat way too much. Then we skip dinner.

We started our Happy Hour tradition the first time we lived in Mexico. Before that time, we worked and didn't have the time to have a Happy Hour. After arriving in Mexico, we realized that all our old rules, habits, and traditions were no longer viable. We could start new ones. So, we did.

Having Happy Hour in Mexico is very easy. Meals are different in Mexico. We eat a light breakfast, then a substantial meal (*comida*) at around 2 or so in the afternoon, followed by a light dinner a few hours later. Happy Hour is often our dinner, especially after a heavy *comida*. Mexico was made for this kind of flexibility.

In our first Happy Hour repast in Mexico, we just had cheeses and meats, with a cocktail. We've since expanded our offerings.

I like to grill some bread, swipe it with a slice of garlic and then a bit of olive oil. Sometimes I have grilled peppers to place on the bread, with or without cheese. I usually grill the peppers while I'm grilling dinner. I char the peppers, put them in a plastic bag, and then peel the skin off.

I also like to roast cherry tomatoes. They are also very sweet and delicious when put on grilled bread.

Lately, I'm into tapenade. I love it on the grilled bread with a thin slice of the roasted peppers on top.

One of our favorite Happy Hour treats is Guacamole. I also like to make hummus with crackers or toasted pita bread. Our all-time favorite treat is *gougeres*: tasty bite-sized cheesy balls.

The Eater

Click-bait articles on the internet are getting more desperate by the day. I saw one recently that had a photo of Brooke Shields. The headline shouted: "Brooke Shields' 12-year-old daughter looks just like her." Now, why did they think I would click through to see what her daughter looks like when they've already shown me? I could look at the photo of Brooke Shields in the article and know the answer. However, if that headline had read: "Brooke Shields' 12-year-old daughter looks like Danny DeVito," I'm clicking through in a nanosecond.

You might be thinking what does Danny DeVito have to do with Happy Hour? Nothing, unless he's hosting one and picking up the tab. But I did some research on Happy Hour so you wouldn't have to and the results are worth, well, let's just say I think the results are worth toasting.

The exact origin of the expression "Happy Hour" is unclear. As a former member of the United States Navy, however, I am pleased to report that one credited origin comes from shipboard life. In 1913, sailors aboard the USS Arkansas called their semi-weekly smokers the "Happy Hour

Social." (Similar names had been used by women's social clubs since the late 19th century.) By the end of World War I, the entire Navy was holding such gatherings. No wonder we won the war to end all wars.

During the Prohibition era, the concept of drinking before dinner really took off. Your typical speakeasy became a popular haunt for those wishing to drink before eating at a restaurant where alcohol was prohibited, marking the birth of the modern cocktail lounge.

If we fast forward to a *Saturday Evening Post* article in 1959, we learn that the term "Happy Hour" was being used by the U.S. military to describe afternoon drinks in a bar. Apparently, many government contractors and military personnel liked their afternoon get-togethers while stationed in the Atlantic and Caribbean. Who wouldn't? Several other refences to "Happy Hour" had occurred in print years earlier, mostly from places near Naval bases in California. It's not just a job, it's a Happy Hour.

The Happy Hour concept had a limited impact on my life until I retired. Before that, we'd occasionally meet friends after work at a local bar for cheap drinks and small plates. But after a long day at work and usually facing a long commute back home, we didn't exactly party-hearty during the late afternoon hours between four and six.

All of that changed with retirement. We'd invite friends over to our house for Happy Hour, go to their house for the same, or meet at a bar. Little did we know that was the beginning of our descent down a slippery slope. With no

job to commute to or from, we began the unhealthy habit
of sitting in front of our TV, eating and drinking two hours
before we were to sit down at our dining table for a supper
that included more eating and drinking. My once-muscular
frame became portly in no time at all. The advent of the
pandemic blasted this unhealthy sedentary habit into the
Danger-Will Robinson zone.

Today, thanks to platters of cheeses and meats, and small
bites made by Arlene, such as her incredibly delicious gougères
(French cheese puffs), potato knishes, pepperoni rolls, crostini,
and caprese salad, I look like a guy who swallowed a New
England lobster diver and forgot to cough him back up.

The other downside for me with Happy Hour is, when
I experience too much of it, I am not as hungry as I should
be when dinner is served. And, as they say in the culinary
world, hunger is the best sauce.

Yet I persist. I gladly still participate in such diversions,
in spite of my circumference.

Pre-pandemic, we would meet friends on Taco Tuesday at Hank's (formerly Harry's) in the Centro district of
San Miguel. The popular bar, billed as a New Orleans Cafe
& Oyster Bar, starts its Happy Hour at 5 P.M. and runs it
for three hours. Exactly at five in the afternoon, the place
cranks up a song to the decibel-level of a jet engine, an-
nouncing the beginning of another raucous evening. Each
day might offer a different two-for-one drink special, but
on Taco Tuesday, it's always a margarita. On that day, crispy
Taco Bell-like tacos are also added to the bar menu.

The first time we lived in San Miguel, Arlene worked one day a week as a volunteer copy editor for the local bilingual weekly newspaper. On that day, I'd pick her up before 5 P.M. and we'd wander over to Harry's (now called Hank's) for drinks. One afternoon, we walked in and asked if Happy Hour had started. The waitress said yes and told us to hurry. For a few minutes, instead of 2-for-1, she explained, it was 4-for-1. Apparently, the bartender had just lost a game of liar's dice to a customer, and the house was on the hook for double the usual discount.

We took a taxi home.

Cooking and Eating in Mexico

No nachos. No chimichangas.
No Blueberry-Hibiscus margaritas.
Are you sure we're in Mexico?

The Cook

In 2005, Mark and I, along with our black Standard Poodle and sassy cat, sold everything, packed up the car and moved to the Central Highlands of Mexico, San Miguel de Allende, to be exact.

Basically, we dropped out. And then, two years later, we dropped back in and moved back to the States.

Fast forward three years and there we were again, in San Miguel de Allende. Then back to the States one more time. We are back now in San Miguel, and I have no intention of leaving Mexico again.

San Miguel, as most places, changed while we were gone. It is now a UNESCO World Heritage site and a major tourist destination. To accommodate these tourists, the town has become a foodie destination.

We have a once-a-week Organic Farmer's market, as well as a number of organic, gourmet food shops. A lot of new, innovative restaurants have opened. Now in San Miguel, you can go out for Mexican—both traditional and updated—Italian, Thai, Indian, Brazilian, Chinese, Peruvian, and Argentinean food.

I can go to a gourmet shop and buy locally-made cheeses, fresh tofu, hand-made tahini and a variety of curry pastes, as well as fresh, locally-made sausages. I can get just about every spice that someone can get in the U.S.

So, what do I do with all this? I cook. And I have dinner parties.

Because we have near-perfect weather here, I can entertain outside just about all year. During the day, even in winter, the temperature is about 75 degrees F. In summer, the temperature is usually about 85 degrees. This is great weather for a barbeque and that's what we do. I make paella on the barbeque, as well as chicken under a brick. And, of course, pizza baked on the grill.

For our first Thanksgiving back in Mexico, I planned a party. We set up tables in the back courtyard, invited lots of friends, and I started cooking. Turkey is easy to find in Mexico. In fact, I think turkey (*pavo* in Spanish), is indigenous to this country. At least, they sure love their *pavo*. Cranberry sauce—canned or fresh—is a bit more difficult. You can find it, but you pay a premium. I always pay the price. Potatoes are also tricky. White potatoes are easy and plentiful, but russet or other potato types are almost non-existent. Why? I have no idea. There are plenty of fresh vegetables to choose from; they are very easy to find and delicious. What about pumpkin pie? I bought it!

It was a great party that went on for many hours. Friends who had other plans stopped by for a late dessert. People ate, stayed, left, then were replaced by late-arriving friends.

The party went so well that we decided to do a big party for Christmas. As you can imagine, Christmas is a big deal in Mexico. There are posadas and pinatas and parties and parades. There were three sets of expats living in a line on the same street. We thought it would be fun to have a progressive dinner. Mary, who was the first house in the line, did the first course and cocktails. We were the middle house so we did the main course. Kate, in the last house, did the dessert.

We didn't really think it through. We all invited friends, so there were about 100 people. They arrived at Mary's house between 6 and 7 P.M. This was great since their arrival was a bit staggered. At 7 P.M., they ALL arrived at our house. The line stretched out to the street, looking like a bread line. And they were hungry, very hungry.

I thought I had cooked enough: a Mexican Cassoulet, grilled vegetables, three kinds of roast pork, and more. In 15 minutes, the table was empty. All the food gone!

The party moved to Kate's, but I didn't tag along. I was way too tired.

The next year, we didn't want to, or couldn't, repeat the progressive dinner. So, I had a party for 75 people. We made it an Open House so people didn't come at once. The following year, I trimmed the guest list to 35 people. Our last year, we were down to eleven at Christmas dinner. Manageable and fun.

When back in Oregon, I often reflected on my life in Mexico. Or I should say the parties and food in Mexico.

The Eater

As the assigned eater in this exercise, it is my honor to represent countless others who, like myself, also serve by sitting at a dining table waiting to be served. At this point, I've been asked to say a few words about eating in Mexico, where I now live. I could go on for hours talking about Mexican food. But that would get in the way of my next meal.

Suffice it to say, I can limit my few words to three: Just do it.

Go to Mexico and enjoy one of the world's most imaginative and consistently delicious cuisines up front and personal in its native habitat. Whether you're eating fish tacos on the beach or pork tacos in the mountains, you won't regret it. In fact, in 2010, Mexican cuisine was classified as an Intangible Cultural Heritage of Humanity by UNESCO. How many chances do you get in life to eat an intangible cultural heritage?

Plenty of chances, if you happen to reside in Mexico like I do. One morning in San Miguel, where we lived on a busy street in a mixed-use neighborhood, we stood in front of our gate and a stranger ran up to us. He was out of breath and paused before talking. I imagined he had just arrived, dropped his luggage at the hotel, and raced off to our street. When he gained control of his breath, he asked, "Does that woman who makes those great tamales still live on this street?" We said yes and pointed to a small house almost directly across from ours. And her tamales were not just great, they were fantastic.

I understood his fixation. When we planned our return to San Miguel, I began to crave the chips and salsa at *Hecho en Mexico*, one of our favorite go-to restaurants. What could be so special about your basic chips and salsa, you might ask? Unlike the chips served in many U.S. restaurants, chips so thin you can see through them, the chips here in Mexico are genuine, often made daily by hand, and not by machines processing thousands of chips a minute on a conveyor belt. I wouldn't be surprised to learn that Americans eat more tortilla chips than potato chips.

I love Mexican food—as do many in the United States. In the Western U.S., for example, Mexican food is the most desirable ethnic food; overall in the country, Chinese food is the top choice for most Americans. But it's a close call between the two, with Italian food far behind in third.

America has been called a melting pot, but that pot doesn't just melt what's inside. If the food is Mexican, there is a good chance what is inside is a *mole* simmering all-day to perfection. In the U.S., a *mole* is viewed as a traditional Mexican brown sauce containing chocolate. In reality, there are several *mole* sauces and many of those do not use chocolate.

Mole is a complex dish where, as they say on cooking shows, the sauce is the star, regardless of what protein—if any--is used with it. Not long ago, we were in a restaurant in San Miguel, and Arlene ordered the grilled vegetables with *mole*.

The presentation was a work of art itself: freshly grilled vegetables sitting on top of a round pool of *mole* with a sufficient amount of white plate on the edges to frame the meal. The vegetables were neither diced nor cubed but left whole. Arlene offered me a taste of her dish. I took a few bites, and with every bite I experienced a different spicy taste: chile pepper one time, cinnamon the next. But friends, gourmands, and countrymen, I come to talk about other dishes, not just to praise *mole*.

Now, if you've read this far in our book, you will recognize this is the point in my essay where I list my top five or seven best or ten favorite whatchamacallits. I'm not holding back this time; I'm going for the gold and listing my favorite ten Mexican dishes.

So, here, in alphabetical order, are the ten Mexican dishes I enjoy eating the most (cue the Mariachi band):

Chilaquiles. This is a dish that answers the age-old question about what to do with all those leftover tortilla chips from last night's fraternity party. Put them at the base of a pan, pour salsa over them, melt cheese over the dish, and add pieces of chicken to the pan or an egg to the top. Or don't worry about which came first—the chicken or the egg — and include both. I love this dish for breakfast.

Chile relleno. Okay, here's another dish I love for breakfast, as well. It's typically a poblano *chile* stuffed with cheese, coated in a simple corn flour, and fried. We sometimes eat it for lunch or just a midday snack.

Guacamole. As a guac lover, I can eat guacamole any time of day or night. Who knew? A little girl from Long Beach, Long Island, New York, named Arlene makes one of the best guacamoles I've ever tasted.

Mexican wedding cookies. I love butter cookies, and these tasty little morsels are exceptional. Granted, Mexico offers other dessert options, from flan to churros, but I love the simplicity of these cookies. Fair warning: they can be addictive.

Pozole. This is my latest favorite Mexican dish, and I know I've already praised its edible charms—but, in my opinion, it is worth repeating. *Pozole* is a traditional pre-Hispanic corn broth or stew, which may not sound like much but it punches well above its weight class. I can't seem to get enough of this dish. According to anthropologists, the original protein was human, often warriors who came out on the losing end and became a protein to be named at a later date. Instead of being shipped to the minor leagues, they were consumed. Once pigs arrived in the New World, pork replaced homo sapiens as the protein *du jour* (good call, I might add). *Pozole* is usually made in a clay pot with hominy and other ingredients. There are a multitude of *pozoles* in Mexico. When ready, the dish is served with several side condiments, including small bowls of lettuce, chopped onion, avocado, radish, cheese, and cilantro. Arlene doesn't add the tortilla chips to the broth because they get too soggy. Instead, she serves them in a bowl, along with the other additions.

Arroz con frijoles. I doubt I needed to list rice and beans, but I love the combination—the yin and yang—of Mexican side dishes. I guess I could have listed *enchiladas* instead of rice and beans, but I wanted to give a shout-out to the supporting cast. And a separate hats-off to freshly made tortillas, quickly fried on a flat griddle known as a *comal*.

Sopa azteca (aka tortilla soup). It's been said that in the screenwriting business, a producer might remind a writer about a popular movie, telling the writer to come up with something like it only different. And that is how I would describe *sopa azteca*, a Mexican soup similar to *pozole* but different. I love both.

Tacos. Arlene could easily make and I could just as easily eat tacos for every meal. One of her specialties is chicken tacos with her own sauce and topped with thin, pickled red onions.

Tamales. Tamales in Mexico are often consumed mid-morning as a snack. But, here again, I'll eat any tamale put in front of me, any time of day or night.

Two Mexican foods I'm trying to like but can't get there yet are *huitlacoche* and *chapulines*. The first is sometimes referred to as a Mexican truffle; it's a fungus on ears of corn. I'm willing to admit, the last time I had *huitlacoche* over grilled bread it was delicious. So, it looks like I'll be joining the fungus fan club soon.

The second dish, *chapulines,* consists of dried and roasted grasshoppers. Unfortunately, I am not planning to apply for membership to the *Chapulines* Eaters Support Group in the near-term. I'm afraid they'll have to hold their annual convention again this year without me.

If It Tastes So Good, Why Should I Feel Guilty?

So, there's a burglar in the kitchen. If he eats
your fruitcake, he'll drop dead on the spot.

The Cook

During our second stay in Mexico for five years, we had a rotating set of friends over to watch movies. We would send out an email, letting everyone know what movie we would be showing, and anywhere from 6 to 20 or more friends would show up. Because we didn't ask for an RSVP, we never knew how many people would show up. This was part of the fun!

We had a social hour, starting at 6 P.M., with the movie starting at 7 P.M. We called it "Guilty Pleasures" because these were fun movies. Not serious, but fun. In other words, a guilty pleasure.

Everyone who came was asked to bring something to drink and something to share. The "something to share" ranged from store-bought chips and dip to homemade tortilla cups, filled with beans and cheese to rice crispy cakes. We always had an array of beverages: wine, gin, vodka, tequila (this is Mexico, after all) and soft drinks. And beer, of course.

Really, a potluck that surpassed all potlucks.

I really didn't do a great deal of cooking for this event. But I always put out chips and salsa. Mark made popcorn.

What's a movie without popcorn? Sometimes I bought spiced chicken wings (they were bright RED!) at the Tuesday open-air farmers' market. I roasted or barbecued them, served with a sour cream dip.

I often cooked up a batch of deviled eggs. Everyone loves deviled eggs.

Movies are really Mark's guilty pleasure. Not mine. Crowds of people coming to the house every month, month after month after month, is not my ideal notion of a good time. My guilty eating pleasure is eating potato chips with a diet coke, which was my school lunch for much of my growing up days. (I hate cafeteria food so I ate from the vending machine at school. Truth be told, I still hate cafeterias. They smell awful.)

My cooking guilty pleasure is making fritters. Any kind. When I was a poor graduate student and living in Reno, I made fritters of leftover mashed potatoes, some hamburger meat, and vegetables. I would add an egg, maybe some flour or bread crumbs, fry in some oil. Voila! Dinner.

I like making fritters because I can be creative. And they are a great comfort food for me. My mother used to make a fritter consisting of mashed potatoes and canned peas and carrots (remember them: nicely diced and tasteless.) Let's face it, anything even slightly fried is good.

Now, of course, being the foodie that I am, my fritters are more upscale. Salmon cakes (really a dressed-up fritter), crab cakes, zucchini fritters (useful when you have a vegetable garden overflowing with zucchini) and the ever-popular corn fritters. When I was young and married to my first husband, I made corn fritters with canned cream corn. I'm sort of embarrassed to say that they were quite tasty.

I make Mark corn fritters now from fresh corn. He remembers them from his childhood, topped with maple syrup.

My other cooking guilty pleasure is puff pastry. At one time, in my younger days, I made puff pastry from scratch. I would not recommend doing that. Ever.

One of the great joys—and there are plenty—of living in Mexico is that most bakeries, as well as supermarkets, sell puff pastry.

The uses for puff pastry are endless. I make beef wellington (a special treat) with it. During the pandemic, when we were in Oregon, I made individual chicken pot pies crowned with puff pastry. I would make six at a time and freeze them.

I make my version of knishes with puff pastry and sausage encased in the pastry. Making the knishes is easy. I have made them with leftover mashed potatoes and also with store-bought ones. Season the potatoes; roll out the pastry so that it is thin, cut into three- or four-inch squares, plop some mashed potatoes in the center, then fold the pastry around the potatoes. Dip each knish into an egg wash and bake at 375-degrees (more or less) for 20-25 minutes. Sprinkle with some salt and serve with mustard. These freeze very well and are great for parties.

If I have fruits that have seen better days, especially berries, I make hand pies or turnovers with them. Here, again, the process is easy: sprinkle the fruits with some sugar, maybe some grated lemon peel, and let sit for a few minutes. Roll out the pastry and then cut it into large squares. Spoon the fruit in the middle, fold the pastry around the fruit, and sprinkle the top with cinnamon sugar. Bake for 20-25 minutes and your dessert will be ready.

Now that I think about it, fritters and puff pastry are very similar. They involve taking bits and pieces and making something delicious out of them. It is creative and I don't know why I consider them a guilty pleasure.

Creativity should never be a guilty pleasure.

The Eater

So, I take it we're talking about the usual ballyhoo about guilty pleasures? I can go there. I was raised Catholic, so I know a little something about guilt. To save time, however, I'll limit myself to the following ten, even though I have many more, trust me:

Pizza. Look, everyone loves pizza. Right? Especially, since it now comes with gluten-free and vegan options. If visitors from another planet came down here for a long weekend, and I wanted to help make their vacation memorable, I'd take them to get a slice. They might like it enough to order an extra-large pizza to go.

Still, I have rules. I'm not too fussy about my toppings. I possess the traditionalist's deep-seated aversion to pineapple on my pizza, of course, and I'm just now getting accustomed to anchovies.

However, where I draw the line is in the crust. Sorry, Chicago, but I'm not a fan of the kind of deep dish you're known for, a doughy pizza that's so thick and deep it could hide a Volkswagen. I believe too much dough spoils the crust, not to mention the toppings. If I wanted to eat bread,

I would order a loaf. If I wanted to eat a pie, I'd order a pie. But when I want to eat pizza, give me whatever passes for a thin New York slice any day of the week--especially with pepperoni on the top. (Another one bites the crust. Arggh).

Deli meats & cheeses. For little bites to share with visitors, I love nothing more than a platter of processed meats and cheeses, especially mortadella and salami; just about any cheese will do, as long as it doesn't come in a jar or a toothpaste tube. The platter would, of course, include a mix of nuts and olives.

Spoiler alert. I'm one of those irredeemable selfish types who will pick all the cashews from a bowl and leave the peanuts behind.

I prefer my olives with pits because they seem to taste better. I don't understand why, they just do. My favorite is Castelvetrano olives, which were originally from Sicily but are now grown elsewhere, just not in my back yard. They require a dry, intense heat. A Castelvetrano olive is green, larger than most, tasty, and meaty. Some consider it the best olive in the world. I know I do.

Fast Food. Okay, this one's easy. How can one not feel guilty about eating fast food, especially when the food is a life-shortening timebomb, and the franchises don't pay their employees anything close to a living wage?

It's the pleasurable part of the equation that's harder to detect. I generally keep away from fast food, for health reasons and to avoid unnecessary strife in my marriage. But if I'm on my own and without any "adult" supervision, I will often choose one of two guilty pleasures. I will either go for the crunchy tacos served at Taco Bell or the fried chicken from Popeye's.

Licorice. Please, no weird flavors like watermelon or peach or cilantro. I'm old fashioned and want my licorice to look and taste like licorice, either black or red. Back in the day, I was known for going through an entire bag of licorice on my own, albeit a small bag. It's an acquired skill and taste. These days, I mostly stay away from licorice, after reading about a 54-year-old man who died because he ate too much of it. According to the FDA, the candy contains glycyrrhizic acid, a sweetener that may cause high blood pressure and heart failure.

In small amounts, licorice is harmless. So, when I want to be bad and go off of whatever diet I'm miserably failing, I might buy a box of Bassatt's Allsorts, a candy mix created in England around 1899 by accident. As the story goes, a candy salesman was carrying a tray of sweets to show a customer, tripped, and fell, mixing the candies up. The customer liked the mixture and licorice history was made. When I buy Allsorts these days, I limit myself to two or three pieces a day.

Fennel has a licorice-like flavor, which makes it an acceptable, healthy substitute. Arlene likes to cook with fennel, which is good news for me. Plus, we both enjoy sambuca, as an after-dinner drink, and never feel guilty about it. Although I may no longer be buying whips, ropes, or buttons of licorice, I've found other ways to compensate.

Hot dogs. In 2020, Joey 'Jaws' Chestnut broke his own hot dog eating world record by consuming 75 frankfurters at one sitting. What is wrong with that man? I love hot dogs, but you can put me down for two, and I'm still going to need to take an antacid. Whenever we go to Costco, buying one of their hot dogs is a treat, a treat I always feel guilty about twenty minutes later. But you won't find me driving the Oscar Mayer Wienermobile or stealing its hubcaps. I'm more of a Hebrew National dog fan. I mean, how can you not love a hot dog that claims to answer to a higher authority?

Cookies. My all-time favorite cookie is the basic shortbread cookie. Living in Mexico, we've become fond of what's known as Mexican wedding cookies, a butter cookie variation sometimes called a snowball.

For the holidays, I used to make a sugar-coated ginger snap but made sure to keep it too soft to snap, crackle, or pop. I prefer my snaps chewy, with a noticeable molasses kick. I also like chocolate chip cookies. Yet not all chocolate chip cookies are equal, mind you. Again, I prefer the soft, chewy ones to the hard as ceramic plate versions. I know the harder ones are designed for dunking, but it's not as if I carry a glass of milk with me wherever I go. The soft cookies, on the other hand, don't need an intervention. And I prefer the larger freshly-made cookie to the smaller ones sold in boxes at the local store.

I find cookies hard to resist, so we usually no longer keep them in the house. And if they happen to sneak into our house, they don't stay long. Cookies, can't live with 'em and, well, you know the rest.

Chicken fried steak. When we're on the road and stopping by a highway diner for breakfast, I have no choice but to order chicken fried steak, with biscuits and gravy. In fact, it's the only time I'm allowed to order it. And if they're out of that dish, I'll opt for corned beef hash, which, truth be told, is not a private guilty pleasure since Arlene will usually share the hash with me. However, she won't go near chicken fried steak with a ten-foot fork.

Corn Pops. This is a pleasure I enjoy for breakfast, but only at home. I am not about to pay an inflated charge for eating dry cereal in a restaurant when I am fully capable of opening a cupboard, removing a box of cereal, pouring it into a bowl, and adding milk all on my own. Don't try this at home, kids. I'm professionally trained.

Popcorn. Speaking of Corn Pops (how's that for a corny segue?), popcorn remains one of my favorite pleasures. I stick to the basics: popcorn, a little butter, even less salt these days. I don't make Cajun-spiced or caramel-covered popcorn. Best of all, it can be made in three minutes in the microwave; which, I know, includes a higher percentage of fat than if cooked on the stovetop. But, still, come on. Three minutes!

Unless you're like my wool-gathering college roommate, who preferred to use the stovetop instead of the microwave. Unfortunately, he forgot to put the lid on. Popped corn flew at us from all directions, as if an army inside of the pot was furiously lobbing grenades. Since then, I've always made mine in the microwave.

You can always tell when I've been eating popcorn and where I was sitting. In my wake, the floor is covered with popcorn detritus, signs of a decaying civilization. Or, as Arlene has asked many times, how can I miss my own mouth? She's right. After so many years of my head staying essentially in the same place on my neck, I still have problems finding my mouth. It's a gift.

Wine in a box. Instead of a guilty pleasure, this might be more appropriate under the category of The Guy Who Invented This Should Be in Jail. It is dangerously easy to open the refrigerator door, press a button on the box, and get a refill. Unlike pouring wine out of a bottle, which gives you an ongoing visual display of how much you are consuming and when it's time to stop, whatever remains in that box is hidden from view. That is, until the box is empty, forcing you to go to the store to buy another one. It's a devious marketing ploy, and I fall for it every time.

Dining in Restaurants

Would you like me to wrap up the rest
of your meal to take home?

The Cook

My mother was a waitress—a great waitress. Through her eyes, I gained an appreciation of what it takes for a restaurant to produce great food and a wonderful dining experience. Restaurants have a very high failure rate and it is easy to understand why.

The food may be great, but the person sitting at the table next to you is loud and obnoxious. Or, your car is broken into while you are eating. Or a hundred other things that have nothing to do with the food and everything to do with your dining experience.

You may question why I have an essay about restaurants in a book about cooking, at least my part about cooking. Well, first off, eating in restaurants provides a learning opportunity. A cook can see what's trendy, learn about a new dish or flavor combination. As a cook, it's great to eat someone else's cooking.

And, also, because many people entertain in restaurants, rather than cook. They may have a small apartment, or don't cook, or some other rational reason to not entertain at their home, but in a restaurant.

I kind of like the idea of entertaining in a restaurant. You don't have to deal with a mess in the kitchen and the cleanup afterwards. Someone else does the cooking and the dishes. During the meal, you can talk and laugh and party with your guests, oblivious to any kitchen disasters—real or imagined.

Sometimes, in odd moments or when I'm bored, I think about what my ideal dining restaurant would be like.

It would be close to home so I could walk to dinner and walk back home. Of course, the weather would always co-operate and be a bit crisp, yet dry.

My ideal restaurant would be a welcoming place. I would be greeted like an old friend upon arrival, perhaps with a hug and a peck on the cheek. The wait staff would know that I want a cold dry gin martini, but would always ask, never assume.

The restaurant would always be busy, although not too busy to get me a table on a moment's notice. It would be a happy place, bustling with activity so I felt young and care-free when I dined there and when I brought guests there.

The food in my ideal restaurant would be comfortable, yet varied enough so I wouldn't get bored. It would be a place where I could try the latest food trends, yet always have the basics.

When I invite guests to my favorite restaurant, they would be treated like royalty, and I would be the center of the event.

When I go to my favorite restaurant, Cafe Firenze, here in San Miguel, the owner—Antonio—greets me with a kiss on the check. The head waiter, Carlos, does also. This makes me feel special even though I suspect that they do that to everyone. Carlos always comes to our table and chats a bit, asking how we are. This always impresses out-of-town visitors.

In New York, my favorite restaurant, until it closed, was Gran Ticino. They didn't greet me as impressively as Cafe Firenze, but they always seemed to remember me.

When Mark and I visited Greenwich Village together for the first time after I had been gone for five years, we went to one of my favorite restaurants—the Cookery. The host greeted me as if I had been gone for only a week or so. Mark was very impressed!

When I was very young, in New York, a classmate invited me and my then husband (referred to as Husband #1) to dinner at a restaurant. She was much older—probably 50, which seemed like a 100 to us—and very sophisticated. She lived in Connecticut with her husband, but kept a small apartment in NYC. We had a lovely time.

Okay, I'll tell the whole story. First off, Husband #1 didn't want to go because the dinner interfered with his pot-smoking time. I insisted. Our host brought her "house sitter," who, I think, was her boy toy. I thought that was very urbane and sophisticated. The best thing was that we went to the Minetta Tavern, which was famous then and is even more famous now. (Look it up!).

I have treated friends to lunch, but can't remember ever hosting a party in a restaurant. I'm too much of a cook and a scaredy cat. It seems that as soon as you recommend a restaurant, a friend goes and has a truly horrible meal there. It must be a rule of the universe.

However, eating in restaurants doesn't always mean entertaining friends there. Sometimes it means eating alone and entertaining yourself. I love eating alone in restaurants and have never understood why some people don't like it.

I traveled a bit for business and instead of ordering room service, as many of my fellow travelers did, I would go out to a nice restaurant and order a meal that my per diem would cover.

I usually started with a martini, especially if the restaurant was within walking distance of my hotel. Then I would peruse the menu carefully and order. I always had dessert. I never brought a book to read. I wanted to concentrate on my dinner and the people around me. It is always a joy to watch people when you're alone and have no one sitting beside you to pay attention to.

When I was in graduate school in Reno, Nevada, and very poor, I would treat myself at the end of each semester at one of the better restaurants in town. I always went alone. It was a fish restaurant, which should have scared the bejesus out of me since Reno is in the desert. But I had lived on both coasts and missed seafood so much that I was willing to risk food poisoning for a taste of the sea.

I always started with escargot, which was one of their specialties. I didn't have a martini—I didn't start drinking them until much later in life—but probably had a nice scotch and water. Then wine with dinner.

Entertaining yourself is sometimes the most entertaining.

The Eater

Dining in restaurants? The short answer is yes. I like to dine in restaurants. Where should we go? More importantly, who's picking up the tab? I'm on a tight budget these days.

Dining in a restaurant may not always be what it seems. So, it helps to agree on a definition. Allow me to explain. Prior to starting college, I worked swing shift as a busboy at the Mapes Hotel in downtown Reno. It was then that I first noticed the dual concept of dining in restaurants.

The hotel dining room was on the first floor; the kitchen was in the basement. I would clear tables, then wheel a cart full of dirty dishes into a service elevator, go to the basement, and push the over-laden cart to where it would be cleaned by some guy, sweating like vegetables in a pan of oil. Although my job was simple, his job was just as simple but harder. I'd unload the dirty dishes from my cart to his conveyor belt. He would scrape the leftover food into a garbage bin, rinse the dishes, and set them inside a huge automatic dishwasher that made as much noise and steam as an old locomotive.

That was the official job description. It didn't work out that way, however, because Dish Washer Guy would pick food from the dirty plates and eat it. Appalling. Disgusting. Check, please! That is NOT dining in a restaurant.

The other kind of dining is the only restaurant dining that truly counts.

As a dedicated eater, dining in restaurants is a huge topic for me, spanning many decades and my waistline. To limit my response and give it a semblance of organization, I'm going to talk about memorable dining moments in different locales, places where Arlene and I lived or visited. With apologies to Julie Andrews, these are a few of my favorite restaurant meals.

Reno, Nevada. Attending college in a casino town had its advantages. It was easy to find a job to fit your class schedule, with three shifts running twenty-four hours a day. Best of all, friends who worked in casinos were always willing to comp you to a meal. I enjoyed many a free prime rib dinner. At least, I think it was prime rib, but for that price, who knew or really cared? My favorite prime rib restaurant was The Liberty Belle, long since gone, at the southern end of town. Because we were typical college students with cinder block furniture and living month-to-month on a tiny amount of money, dining out wasn't our favorite pastime. On the other hand, thinking about dining out in restaurants became a hobby.

Mountain View, California. It wasn't until we traded academia for high-tech and worked in the Silicon Valley that we could afford and justify dining in restaurants. We both worked long hours and extended those long days by going to school at night. For a period, we took our evening meals at restaurants five times a week, staying home only on the weekend. Fortunately, we lived in Mountain View, near Castro Street, an area famous for its diverse range of restaurants. For Thai, we dined at Bangkok Spoon; for Vietnamese, Mekong. The street had Italian and Chinese and Mexican restaurants. A Salvadoran restaurant, a few streets away, was where we tasted our first *pupusas* and *empanadas*. Closer to our apartment, we could walk to Country Gourmet, a small restaurant where we could enjoy an entrée salad and a glass of wine for under $10. I suspect many of those restaurants are long gone.

Portland, Oregon. When we moved to Portland, in the early 80s, the Rose City was not the foodie city it is today. We lived there for three decades and witnessed the rise of one of the country's greatest food cities in America, much to our dining pleasure. On Saturdays, we would go out for breakfast, logging in time at such spots as Kornblatts, a New York-style deli, and The Heathman Hotel for two different yet fantastic versions of corned beef hash. Sometimes we would eat at The Original Pancake House, which served dollar-sized pancakes and was always busy. Incredible restaurants in Portland are too numerous to mention. And that's not even mentioning Portland's famous food carts, which is not exactly dining in a restaurant, so forget I even mentioned them. I will say, however, my favorite Italian restaurant is Piazza Italia; my favorite restaurant serving Northwest cuisine is Higgins. The beat goes on.

New York City, New York. What's left to say about restaurant dining in New York that hasn't already been said? Meals out are not always as expensive as you might think. A bagel with a schmear for breakfast; a slice of pepperoni pizza for lunch; and dinner out. Okay, that last one is going to cost. Dinners out in New York City are not for the faint of wallet, unless you are eating at a tiny hole-in-the-wall joint in Chinatown.

Still, we are always able to find an amazing meal to fit our budget. We enjoy going to art museums, and when we do, we like to eat in the museum restaurant and have yet to be disappointed. One of our favorite restaurants is Pearl Oyster Bar in the West Village for lobster rolls. And the last time we visited The Big Apple, we enjoyed a delicious paella at Socarrat Paella Bar in Chelsea.

Europe. After three days and nights in London, we discovered the best food in England was not in somber wood-paneled rooms with dark upholstery, served by uniformed waiters pushing silver-domed carts, but in boisterous East Indian restaurants, of which there were many. It was only after we arrived in Paris via the Eurostar train that I came to appreciate French food. As a cook, Arlene, of course, had long ago converted to French cuisine.

We couldn't wait to return to Paris and spend more time, and we did, years later, enjoying ten days of the good life, which included too many delicious meals to list. Sorry.

But I want to mention two restaurants in particular that stood out.

Nearly a decade before the Obamas held their famous date night dinner in Paris at *La Fontaine de Mars*, Arlene and I had dined at that very restaurant twice. We were staying at the Grand Hotel Leveque on Rue Cler Street, a Rick Steves-recommended hotel not far from the Eiffel Tower. La Fontaine de Mars was even closer to where we stayed. I remember it as a classic Parisian bistro, where the locals often outnumbered the tourists.

One evening, we eavesdropped as the American next to our table instructed her friends on the proper way to hold a glass of red wine--by the stem and not the bowl. As she talked, we noticed a nearby table of local Parisians, deep in conversation and wildly enjoying their dinner while holding their wine goblets by the bowl and not the stem. Hmm. How quick the mighty clichés have fallen. Perhaps if you've ordered a bottle of expensive red wine or if you like swirling the contents to make it look as if you're thinking deep thoughts or if you're the one stuck doing the dishes and can't get fingerprints off the glass, then by all means hold the glass by its bottom or stem. No harm, no foul.

My point is this particular restaurant in Paris was a convivial setting, with an appetizing menu and no pretensions. We fully understood why the President and First Lady dined there.

On our last night in Paris, however, we ate at a smaller French bistro, whose name escapes me, not far from *La*

Fontaine de Mars. The joint was jumping, as Fats Waller would say, and we were escorted to the last set of tables, three tables for two, enclosed in its own privacy surround.

One table of the three was already occupied by an elderly British woman, fully dressed for a night on the town and currently reviewing the menu. Her much younger male companion—the woman was his mother's best friend, we later learned — sat across from her. Just as we were preparing to sit down, the older woman, probably hard of hearing, shouted to her companion, in a falsetto voice worthy of a Monty Python skit: "I think I'll have the stuffed quail."

The word "stuffed" was said in a high-pitch, lower only slightly than the word that followed, which was even higher. She lingered on the word "quail," stretching that simple word into a polysyllabic word of her own making. Her voice cut through the din and stopped the three of us — me, Arlene, and the guy being seated next to us — in mid-air. Our butts did not touch the chair for several seconds, as all three of us looked over at the woman. I imagined we shared the same thought: this meal is going to be a lot of fun. And it was.

Hunger might make the best sauce, as the French claim, but, in my experience, companionship makes a great meal even greater.

A Winter's Tale

Summer cuisine always confuses me.
Cold soups and warm salads.

The Cook

Mark thought up this chapter's title. It evokes a sleigh ride through the snow with a bunch of merry people.

Not my thing. I am more like The Winter of our Discontent, keeping with a reference to Shakespeare. I hate the cold and winter is cold. At least where I grew up.

I remember my mother bundling me up so much that I couldn't move, let alone walk. And I was not alone. All of us were so bundled up that we walked around looking like well-dressed zombies. Arms straight out, hats tight over our ears, neon-colored snow suits. We couldn't play; we just stood around.

As a child—a small one at that—I would walk home from school, losing a boot in the snow. I would literally step out of my boot, leaving it behind me in the snow.

Oh, and ice skating. I loved to go to the ice rink. Not for the skating, which I was horrible at, but for the hot chocolate. I eventually stopped skating and just sat—inside—and drank hot chocolate. With marshmallows.

When I was older and living in New York City, I remember standing on a corner waiting for the bus and crying because my feet were so cold. My toes were numb, my hands were stuffed in my coat pocket for warmth, my ears were bright red. I was very unhappy.

In New York, after the snow, there was the slush. Brown snow, with hints of yellow. (Don't even ask!)

If the snow was not enough, there was ice. Slippery, sneaky ice. Walking on ice was horrid but driving on it was even worse.

But, wait! This is about food and cooking and I love winter foods. The warmth of something in the oven, a fireplace glowing, the darkness outside when we eat.

I've always disliked the sun shining when I eat a hearty meal. There's something "off" about it. I love when it is dark out, the table laden with food, candles lit, and friends to share it all.

Winter is made for casseroles, stews, soups; foods that warm the body and soul. Winter is made for cooks.

I love Thanksgiving. Or rather I love the day after Thanksgiving. Turkey sandwiches, topped with stuffing (or dressing), and cranberry sauce, especially the jellied kind that comes in a can. I am in awe of how the rims of the can decorate the cranberry jelly.

And, of course, there is also homemade cranberry sauce. The simplest one is this recipe from Anthony Bourdin. Put a bag of cranberries—or about 12 ounces of fresh, organic ones if you are so inclined—in a food processor with a cut up, scrubbed orange, rind and all. Mix in a cup of sugar and then process. It is delicious. And couldn't be easier.

I am not a person who likes traditions. I get bored with the thought of doing something the same every year. I understand that that is the essence of tradition, but I hate routine and tradition is just a yearly routine.

I hate routine so much that when I worked, I sometimes drove a different route to work or back home. I just couldn't stand the same routine. (Considering that I have no sense of direction, I got lost many times by taking an alternate route. Just another way to step out of my routine.)

That said, Mark and I have a few traditions, especially around the holidays. We spend Christmas Eve and New Year's Eve holidays alone, just the two of us and we cook (together!) a special meal. A winter meal.

It is always nice to spend Christmas Eve with Mark. We cook a special meal, maybe something like a cassoulet (one of Mark's favorites) or coq au vin. We used to open presents, but that tradition has fallen by the wayside. At this time of our lives, we want for very little. Sometimes we buy something "for the house." Something that we both want.

We started the New Year's Eve tradition very early in our marriage as a way to talk about the future and what we wanted from life. During the meal, we talk about the past year and what our goals are for the next one. When we lived in the States, before we retired, my goal every year was to do more creative things—write, do some pottery, etc. It wasn't until we dropped out and left our jobs in 2005 that I actually got to achieve my goals. I can't remember what Mark wanted. Well, enough said about that.

Since we worked long hours, this New Year's Eve tradition gave us a chance to reconnect, talk about the future and eat very well.

We typically started with an appetizer, along with champagne. Very often, Mark had a shrimp cocktail because he loves it. I had caviar because I love it. One year, I made something that both of us liked—Baked Oysters with Snail Butter Encased in Puff Pastry. It was a very nice start to a very nice meal.

One of our favorite main courses for New Year's Eve is Beef Wellington. What could be bad? Filet Mignon topped with mushroom duxelles and encased in Puff Pastry.

I LOVE puff pastry and consider it a matter of national pride that you can buy fresh Puff Pastry from almost every bakery in Mexico, at least where I live in Mexico. How convenient is that? How rational? How delicious!

Dessert is usually something decadent and usually store bought. I am just not up to making dessert. Although we cook this meal together, the major weight of planning and preparation rests on my shoulders.

Did this tradition change with retirement? Yes, a lot. I no longer talk about wanting creative outlets—I do them. Because I cook more and more creatively, it doesn't seem necessary to make a special meal. We have lots of special meals.

But we still sit down, together, just the two of us, every New Year's Eve and talk. Sometimes we make a special meal, but sometimes we order take-out.

I guess some traditions are worth keeping, as long as you change them up.

The Eater

Winter for me is what I call fur-bearing season, a period of time during which I throw my latest diet out into the shivering cold, stay inside where it is warm, and eat more hearty meals, from soups to stews, casseroles to chili con carne. The goal of such conspicuous consumption is to protect my body from the ravages of winter, much like how a musk ox ends up looking so shaggy by late fall. Put another way, it's my version of layering my clothing, only, instead of piling on sweaters and shirts, I'm layering my body, one pound at a time.

This would make perfect survival sense if I were living with a pet musk ox in the Arctic. But I have spent most of my life in very comfortable climate-controlled environments. So, quite frankly, I do not need to generate much fur during the winter; besides, I own plenty of bulky sweaters.

Still, I love winter dining and the concept of growing fur or hair appeals to me, as bonus points, especially since I've been going bald since I was 12. To come full-circle, I look forward each winter to bearing fur, even if it is fake fur. I like to say, I come for the winter season and stay for the meals. Arlene cranks up the cooking volume and serves full-course winter fare including some oldies but goodies as coq au vin, cassoulet, seafood stew, and beef short ribs. She also makes soups, from lentil to potato leek to split pea and ham.

One of my all-time favorite winter dishes is Dungeness crab from the waters of the Pacific Northwest. A simple yet delicious meal can be made of fresh crab, a loaf of sourdough, salad, and chilled white wine. If we have any crab leftover, Arlene makes crab cakes that are delicious as breakfast or appetizers. And as you might have guessed, I like crab cioppino and will often order it, if the dish is on the menu.

Many years ago, we attended a crab cioppino feast in St. Helena, California, where my parents lived at the time. The event was held at the local Grange and my dad was one of the organizers. We drove up from San Jose, a trip of about two hours. At the end of the evening, there was so much cioppino left over that they gave us a huge container of it to take home. That was the good news. The bad news? The container tipped over and the car's interior smelled like crab from that point on, despite our best efforts of scrubbing the crime scene. Whenever we would turn on either the heater or the air conditioner, the "shellfishy" air made us feel as if we were floating in crab bisque. When it came time to sell the car, we had to wait until the weather outside was moderate, not too cold or too hot, and didn't require turning on the airflow.

November is when I leave grazing behind and trade it in for some serious, heads-down eating. Two food-related dates are always on our calendar at that time of year: my birthday and Thanksgiving, and both are usually mere days apart.

The hidden challenge, if not curse, of being a talented cook, such as Arlene, is that it is harder to justify dining out in a restaurant, when she cooks such delicious meals at home. I know, I know. It is not fair to Arlene. And, yes, we still love dining out but are very picky these days, especially in retirement with less income. For example, we will dine out if it's a special occasion with friends or if the restaurant serves a cuisine not cooked at home, such as Peruvian. Simply put, Arlene cooks better meals than most meals we've had in restaurants. It's a good problem to have, if you're the eater in this family drama.

Every year when my birthday rolls around, Arlene makes a meal of my choice. Upon special request, she will sometimes make me a rack of lamb, served with grilled asparagus and her incredible *au gratin* potatoes. For dessert, she'll pick up either a pecan pie or cheesecake.

More often than not, my birthday meal is spaghetti carbonara, a pasta dish from Rome. Sometimes it's called Italian bacon and eggs and for good reason: pasta (usually spaghetti but other pastas may be used), egg (tricky because you don't want to end up with scrambled egg), hard cheese (parmesan), cured pork (pancetta or bacon), and black pepper. Arlene makes it with cream, which might vary from the traditional recipe but ends up making the dish creamy.

And—insert popup message alerting you to a forced segue coming—speaking of spaghetti carbonara, did you know that Calvin Trillin, the famous food writer and humorist, for decades has been waging a campaign to replace turkey with spaghetti carbonara for Thanksgiving? It's such an obvious win-win. Those celebrating the holiday enjoy an incredibly delicious meal and, at the same time, are spared the indignity of watching the President of the United States of America pardon two senseless turkeys named Frick and Frack from getting chopped. Sign me up.

I believe I can state without fear of contradiction that Thanksgiving is Arlene's favorite day for cooking. If she had her druthers, we would always spend it at home and she'd do the cooking. But life doesn't always follow the druthers theory, and since Arlene believes the best part of a tradition is doing something different than expected, we have spent Thanksgiving in a range of settings outside of our own home: restaurants in Portland, Las Vegas, or New York City, say, or on a commercial airflight, or at a friend's house. All tasty, all memorable.

When we roll into December, we have two big meals on the horizon: Christmas and Hanukah. The former might feature a ham dinner with potatoes *au gratin*; the latter often is a time for potato latkes and brisket.

On the last night of December, aka New Year's Eve, we follow our only tried and true tradition as spouses. We stay

home and cook a special meal together. With the meal prepared and served, we sit at our dining table, adulting, one
might say, with lighted candles and music and drinks (a
martini for Arlene, wine for me). We talk about the year that
just passed and the year ahead. We started this tradition
many years ago when we were both working long hours
and rarely seemed to just sit and talk. We would choose a
cuisine we rarely cook or eat, such as a New Orleans-style
meal or a New England-style meal.

As I emerge from the fog of winter dining, I can see a
rainbow ahead. At its end is a pot of corned beef simmering, smelling better than a pot of gold. March 17 is next. Arlene makes a delicious corned beef, and oven roasts, rather
than boiling, the vegetables. If you've never had cabbage
oven-roasted with corned beef, you are in for a treat.

Lucky me, eh?

Gone Grillin'

That's not a burger, it's a briquet!

The Cook

I am not a big fan of barbequing or grilling for parties. It is just too last minute for me. Not to mention all the smoke, all the people poking at the fire and meat. It is just too invasive for me.

It always seems that as soon as I start to put the food on the barbecue, some guy comes along to tell me how to do it. It is usually someone who doesn't know how to cook, but thinks he is a master griller. I am convinced that all men think they can grill. I always ignore them, of course. Most of the time, men who grill, but don't really cook, grill the life and taste out of the food. Hamburgers like hockey pucks; salmon blackened beyond repair; steak too well-done. We've all been victims of men at the barbecue. I am so sorry.

I have found a couple of barbecue meals that are okay for parties. Paella is a great dish made on the barbecue and fairly easy. Living in Mexico, we are surrounded by not only Mexican cooking, but Spanish cooking. And, to me, Spanish cooking is all about paella. I've made paella in a skillet on the top of the stove, but I wanted to make it the "real" way—on the grill.

The trick to great paella is to cook almost all of it before-hand. And then just do the rice on the barbecue. You end up looking like a Grilling Diva. The day before the party, I grilled the chicken thighs and the shrimp. About an hour before our friends came over, I steamed the mussels and clams in chicken broth laced with saffron. While we sat in our courtyard, having cocktails and marinated mush-rooms, we got the grill going.

Somewhere in this vast internet world is a video of me, cooking paella for the first time on the barbecue in Mexi-co. It was hot; it was fun; it was very tiring. But the paella turned out perfect. We did this party numerous times, al-ways to great success.

I have also made large rib-eye steaks on the grill. I make a variety of sauce toppings (gorgonzola is a favorite) for the meat. The nice thing about a rib-eye steak is that you can slice it and then serve it at room temperature.

I have grilled oysters on the barbecue, and they are spec-tacular. It is difficult to believe, but we can get oysters in the middle of Mexico. Don't ask me how, or for any particulars, but we get oysters. I wouldn't attempt to eat them raw so I decided to cook them, both in the oven and on the barbecue.

We gathered about ten or so friends for an oyster party. I made snail butter, which is a mixture of garlic, parsley and butter that can make anything, even an old shoe, tasty. I put the snail butter on the opened oysters and laid them on the grill. It doesn't take long for the butter to melt and the oysters to cook.

I also cooked oysters in the oven. Okay, okay, I know this is a chapter on grilling, but cut me some slack. I deserve it.

When writing about grilling, the question that invariably comes up is: charcoal or gas? I have used both and like both. During our second stay in Mexico, I used a charcoal grill, heating the coals with a chimney. This was the grill I used to make paella and I think the smoky-ness enhanced the food. In the States, I've always had a gas grill. I don't know why.

Now, back again in Mexico, I bought a Weber gas grill. It is a thing of beauty. To be honest, if I had my druthers, and more room in our courtyard, I would also have a charcoal grill. I really believe that some things just taste better cooked on charcoal.

Maybe soon. We'll see.

The Eater

The definition of barbeque is pretty simple: it's a meal cooked outdoors. But that simple definition hides a complicated history. Let's face it, Man has been cooking meals outdoors since Piltdown Man was in diapers. Picture a caveman wearing a goofy white hat and an apron asking his fellow hunters how they want their mastodon cooked. Rare, I imagine, was the preferred choice.

Oh, wait. Piltdown was a fraud. Forget I even mentioned his name; but you must admit it's still a great name to drop. Let me use a more recent—and scientifically verified—caveman: Ozti the Iceman. You remember him. This is the guy who created quite a stir when he was discovered encased in ice in the mountains of Switzerland in 1991. Apparently, Ozti died 4,000 years ago; one blanches at the thought of the hotel bill he must have left behind. And no—he didn't look like Brendan Fraser. He looked more like Willie Nelson.

A sentence in an online article I read recently asked, "What did cavemen eat to make them so healthy?" I think the word healthy might be a stretch. I can go with the word survive. Ozti died in his late 40s, but he lived during the

Age of Copper (I seriously doubt he would have known enough about marketing to assign his life an Age, but that's history for you). With an average life expectancy for the earliest cavemen pegged at 25, some of those poor bastards had to endure puberty and a mid-life crisis at the same time. This barely fits my definition of what is required to live a healthy life.

All of this Iceman Cometh background is provided as a prelude to my discussion of grills. You may have heard about or follow the Paleo Diet, a diet designed to resemble what caveman listed on his meal planner. I don't know if that's a good thing or a bad thing. But I am compelled to raise my hand and ask, what's next? The Paleo Fight or Flight Exercise Plan? Paleo Secrets to Closing More Sales? The Paleo Hygiene Program? From skull fragments, we know your typical caveman looked like he had his teeth fixed by a British dentist in the Outback. My history with barbecuing or grilling is much more recent.

Reno, Nevada. When we shared a house with a friend in Reno during college, we bought a small Hibachi grill and made many meals from it on the concrete porch. The kitchen in the house was always dirty, a common trait in college, so we opted for dining al fresco. When the weather cooperated, we enjoyed grilling success. Still, our Hibachi grill could handle only two small burgers cooking at the same time. For an eater, that was a serious limitation.

Portland, Oregon. The first house we purchased in Portland had an outdoor brick grill with a smoker. We were relentless users and began barbecuing more frequently. Just grill, baby. We grilled breakfast. We grilled during snow storms. The outdoor barbecue was a traditional setup, using briquets instead of gas, and the grilling space was more than ample. In our next house, we kept a small Weber off the deck attached to the kitchen.

We built a custom house after that one and added a large Weber gas grill connected to the home's gas line. When it came time to downsize to fit our urban condo, we bought what's called a Patio Caddie Grill, perfectly suited for small and narrow decks. Neither snow, nor rain, nor heat, nor gloom of night kept us from the swift completion of our meals, seven floors above the ground. When we returned from Mexico and landed in southern Oregon, one of our initial purchases was a propane-based grill with plenty of cooking area.

Mexico. This is where our grill story goes slightly off the grate. The first time we lived in Mexico, it was for a period of two years. We bought an artsy-looking metal grill and using it was simple. I would fill a charcoal chimney starter with briquets and newspaper, and then light the grill. After about a thousand attempts, it would get started and we were on our way. The second time we lived in Mexico, we used a charcoal-based grill. The third time, we bought a propane-based Weber. One of my favorite grilled meals in Mexico is whenever Arlene makes paella. On those special occasions, we'd have 5 to 10 others dining with us. Next up, pizza on the grill.

Truth be told, I can eat anything Arlene grills, with the possible exception of creamed corn.

It's My Big Party and
I'll Cry if I Want to

Are you sure the invitation said Tuesday?

The Cook

I love big parties, really love them. I'd rather cook for a big, huge party than a small or medium one. When I talk about a big party, I mean at least 50 to a 100 or so people. A crowd, to say the least.

I like big parties because I can get lost in them. I am a caterer at heart. I like to plan the meal, cook the meal, present the meal, and then disappear. I can stop and chat—very briefly—with a guest and then run off to do one thing or another. It is perfect for an introvert like me!

I also think that big, crowded parties are more fun for the guests. They, too, can chat briefly with a fellow guest and then move on. There are so many people to talk to! And the noise level—high to be exact—conveys excitement and fun.

Cooking for large gatherings takes a great deal of planning. For our almost annual holiday party—typically between Halloween and Thanksgiving—I started making plans in early September. I made lists of the foods that I would cook and a separate list of ones that I would buy.

I always made potato knishes, at least 300, sometimes more. My potato knishes are nothing like the ones I had growing up. (Izzy's Knishes, here's looking at you!) I make my knishes with leftover mashed potatoes, generously seasoned with salt, pepper, garlic powder and onion flakes, folded into puff pastry or crescent dinner rolls. These freeze beautifully.

I also made pepperoni rolls, at least six or seven of them. Both of those I could make a month or so in advance and freeze. This was in the States when I had a spacious refrigerator and freezer.

I always had a nice vegetable platter, along with a cold meat platter. You can buy large quantities of ready-cut vegetables at the local supermarket or Costco. I also bought a variety of desserts—cookies, cupcakes, anything that could easily be picked up—at Costco.

Sometimes I think that my parties were "Catered by Costco." A good cook knows where to buy, as well as how to cook.

There is one dessert that I almost always make: Chocolate Truffles. They are easy to make and much cheaper than buying.

I always had dips—hummus, salsas, and guacamole—with chips. Sometimes I would make chopped liver and, of course, deviled eggs.

If I was very ambitious, I would make salmon rolls. For these, I make a spread of crème fraiche mixed with a bit of sour cream, sometimes some diced red onion, then I cut smoked salmon (lox, really) into small rectangles. I spread a bit of the cream on the lox, top it with a sprig of chive, and roll it up. This is time-consuming, but very tasty.

I also like to take cherry tomatoes and stuff them with some sort of filling.

Since most of our parties were in the late fall or early winter, I would often make a hearty dish, such as Cassoulet. In Mexico, I usually buy a spiral ham and get some small rolls so people can make their own sandwiches.

Although I typically don't serve any cheese at my large parties—no one seems to eat it and it just goes to waste—I do like to make Manchego Squares. Just take a nice Manchego cheese and cut it into 1 inch or so squares. Top each square with a touch of fig or quince jam.

Dates—the kind you eat—are also great for parties. I usually slit them, remove the pit, stuff with an almond sliver, and wrap it up in prosciutto or Serrano ham. Bake for ten minutes or so. It is good hot or room temperature. You can also stuff with blue cheese.

The food is only one aspect of a great party. You need great guests, people who want to enjoy themselves, along with hosts who are relaxed. Do everything ahead and only have a few things that need to be reheated, so you're not spending the whole party in the kitchen.

Enjoy!

The Eater

For two people who consider themselves not very social, we've certainly hosted a lot of social gatherings during our marriage. And as an eater, I could not have been happier. Because most, if not all, of these gatherings included food, starting with our own wedding reception, which Arlene catered to delicious success.

When I first met Arlene, we were both graduate students teaching composition in a university English department. At the time, she was also the cook for a fraternity house, where she fed the boys both lunch and dinner. She only had two rules: no guns on the first floor and the kitchen must always be clean.

One late morning, she arrived at the frat house to see the kitchen was still a disaster. It looked as if a tornado had passed through on its way to Oklahoma. She wrote on the chalk board "Clean up this fucking mess" and walked out. Sorry, guys. No lunch today.

When she returned in the evening to a spotless kitchen, the fraternity president pulled her aside and apologized. He said they had a wild party the night before and everyone had slept in late. It won't happen again, he promised. He also told Arlene she didn't have to use that kind of language.

Maybe she did. It worked. Those party animals cleaned the kitchen.

As it turned out, we are something of party animals, ourselves, even though we are loath to admit it. When living in the Portland metro area, we held an annual winter party that was a big hit. Because it was a buffet and not a sit-down dinner, we made it an open house, with a three-hour window; most people who arrived stayed longer, of course, as is the nature of parties.

One year, we had nearly 120 people attend. That's a whole lot of cooking and eating and drinking and cleaning up after. In addition to an abundance of bottled wines brought by guests, I made the Swedish winter drink *glogg*. There wasn't a dry throat in the house.

It took us a few attempts to get the timing right for our winter open house. If we made it too close to December 25, many people would already have made other plans. After? People were exhausted from going to parties. Too close to Thanksgiving and people were still loading up on antacids. Too late in December and we may have to cancel at the last-minute because of a surprise snow storm. We tried a few different days before settling on a date that would take place after Halloween and before Thanksgiving. We referred to it as our Thanksween or Hallowgiving party. It was a huge success and always a lot of fun.

We continued the tradition after moving back to San Miguel de Allende, Mexico. Our second winter season there, we teamed up with two other neighbors on our street and hosted a holiday progressive dinner. The first house would host a cocktail party. The next would host the dinner. And the third house was to host dessert. Because we were the middle house in the line of houses, we were on the hook for serving the actual meal.

All three houses were allowed to invite guests. Give or take a plate, 100 or so attended. People staggered to show up at the first house, no pun intended, because start times in Mexico are viewed as mere suggestions and not actual clock-times to be honored. But when it was time to move on to the next course—the meal at our house—all 100 were present and accounted for. As a result, a long line extended from our door to the street. Arlene had made an enormous amount of food, to our way of thinking. She was overseeing the meal, while I was in the courtyard serving drinks. Fifteen minutes into the dinner serving, someone getting a drink complained to me, in amazement, that the guests were eating like vultures. I don't recall all the food Arlene made but by the time I went to eat, there was little left but the imagination. As a hungry eater arriving late to the table, I was devasted.

Next winter, the other two houses opted out of doing a progressive dinner, so we held our own winter open house; it was a buffet for 75. The year after that, a buffet for 30. Our last winter there, Arlene cooked an intimate dinner for 11.

If we had stayed any longer, I suspect our big winter party might have been reduced to a table for two. Truth be told, it was rewarding but a lot of hard work, especially for Arlene.

In thinking back to those parties, I enjoyed seeing people I had not seen for a while and catching up. What I enjoyed even more was introducing two of our friends who didn't know each other but, who I felt, had a lot in common and would enjoy each other's company. In business, that act might be called networking, but in one's social life, it's just what friends do.

Just Desserts

Roxanne likes the more refined things
in life: bleached flour and powdered sugar.

The Cook

I love the title of this chapter. When I lived in San Francisco, there was a shop called Just Desserts that served, well, just desserts. What a wonderful idea!

I'm really not much of a dessert person. Okay, I do like chocolate, but I'm quite happy with a chocolate kiss once or twice a day. After dinner, I sometimes like something sweet, a cookie maybe. But I'm not one for a dessert.

I don't consider myself a baker. In fact, I don't like baking and rarely do it. It is too exacting. Cooking is less rule-based and structured. Baking is all about following rules. At least to me. When I worked, I was a process and procedures person. I liked to know that there was a process so that I knew how to break the rules. I guess that is my definition of cooking, but not of baking.

However, when Mark had a play that was being performed at midnight, I thought let's have a pre-theater party of just desserts. I don't usually like themed parties. They remind me too much of matchy-matchy outfits or home décor. These kinds of parties always seem to be trying too hard.

But sometimes a theme is needed, even required. After all, isn't Thanksgiving a themed party? Or Easter? Passover?

And I am almost never still up at midnight, especially for a party. I used to be up for any party. When I was young and living in Manhattan, I would go out at midnight, or even later, to "after-hours" clubs. (They were clubs that opened after the bars closed.) I still can't believe I did that.

But life throws punches and sometimes what seems like a problem ends up being fun! We wanted to get people to attend Mark's play so we decided to have a late-night party and then we could all walk (or drive) over to the theater.

It turned out to be a great party. We started around 9:30 P.M.—a time that most of our friends, including us, are usually getting ready for bed rather than getting ready for a party. We decided that lots of sugar was needed to wake everyone up. So, we decided on desserts—a multitude of desserts.

This party—so different than any we'd ever had—made me think about odd and unusual parties. Sometimes you just have to get over yourself and do something different. Very different. Consider it a leap of faith, or something like that.

The Midnight Dessert Party—as we called it—was one of those parties. But we've had others. (Some would say that the Super Bowl Party was that kind of party for me, but that is a separate topic so I won't go into it here.)

We once had a wonderful Art Gallery Party. An artist friend, who was just starting out, brought some of her paintings over to sell. We hung some and lined more up on the floor. We had appetizers and drinks. She sold some artwork and everyone had a good time.

We had this art party when we first started buying art. Our first piece, called Smiling Again, was an abstract painting of pastel colors. The gallery told us to take it home, hang it and see if we liked it. If we didn't like it, we could return it.

We were in a new house and knew just the wall we wanted it on. We hung the painting, sat on the sofa to admire it, and then watched as it slid down the wall, crashing onto the floor. The glass was broken and the frame slightly bent. We called the gallery and said we loved it, which we did and still do.

At one time, I volunteered to test recipes for a cookbook that was to be published by a local cookware store. I invited some friends over to eat and evaluate the food. I guess you could call it a Food Testing Party.

When we moved to Mexico and I was working on my first book, *Kosher Sutra*, I broadened that party and dubbed it The Oyster Eater.

We gathered together about ten or so friends and had oysters every which way. I grilled them on the barbecue with "snail" butter.

Then I baked some oysters in the oven. I put some snail butter on the top of the oyster, covered the oyster and butter with a thin piece of puff pastry. I baked it until the puff pastry was lightly browned.

For those in the group who did not want oysters, I made shrimp scampi and baked clams. It was quite a party with lots of bread and wine to round out the meal.

Of course, you don't need to have a theme for any party. The best theme to me is The Fun Party.

The Eater

You can probably see my sweet tooth from the international space station or at least from across a crowded room. My sweet tooth may not glow in the dark but it is certainly decaying in fine fashion, as I write these words. The tooth, that is, I don't know the status of the space station. Too much sugar. Again, the tooth, not the space station. A sweet tooth is the curse of the dessert class. Which might explain why I'm rambling. To regroup—slow down, deep breath—where to begin?

I became associated with desserts at an early age. That might serve as my opening statement before Congress, if I were subpoenaed to appear before that august—but mostly useless—political body to give witness to the problem of too much dessert in America. It's a slippery slope. You start with a licorice whip and a Mars Bar as a kid and, before you know it, you're ordering Sambuca and tiramisu for dessert in an Italian restaurant.

And that's how it all started for me: with candy. The day after Halloween was always a day off for those Catholics attending parochial schools. It is officially known as All

Saints Day, but to me, it was All Candies Day. That's because while other kids were in school, I was hanging out with friends and gorging on an assortment of free candy magically pulled from a pillow case.

Pre-healthy lifestyle awareness, we had candy in the house. My mom kept a bowl of candy on an end-table, usually spice drops. Today, the mere thought of eating candy, especially saltwater taffy or an Abba-Zaba bar, makes my teeth shutter with fear. Candy for me now is more likely to come in the form of tropical-flavored Tums.

Fortunately, candy is only a small demographic when it comes to dessert. In contrast to talking about dessert as a whole, which is a huge undertaking (no pun intended). Nonetheless, I shall set my knife and fork aside for the next few minutes and attempt it.

My paternal grandparents in Oakland always had sweet pastries around their house. My grandmother was Swedish and made delicious butter cookies; but she also kept baked treats, including bear claws, butterhorns, marble pound cake, chocolate cream pie, and other sugar-high delights, mostly from Neldam's Danish Bakery, a famous East Bay bakery that closed its doors in 2010.

My mom made a killer cheesecake, and it was her go-to dessert. I can still taste it and relish the memory. My dad, on the other hand, was something of a self-medicating health food nut. His idea of dessert often took the form of wheat germ granules sprinkled over ice cream; and his idea of a refreshing drink, in addition to a cold beer, was Brewer's

Yeast added to cold water and vigorously stirred. Nonetheless, he loved ice cream and his favorite was Maple Nut. For a while as a kid, we made our own ice cream. All I remember about the process is one of us kids would sit on the ice cream machine and take turns churning it using a crank handle. It was summertime, and it kept us busy while the adults partied.

I suppose one cannot truly discuss dessert without first addressing the elephant in the room: chocolate. Like many people, I like chocolate. What more can I say that hasn't already been said about a dessert standard that seemingly works in every culture? From fudge brownies to German chocolate cake to Hershey kisses (which we try to keep in the house, as our only candy vice), it's all appealing. As they say in marketing, chocolate has a long tail. I double-dog dare you to Google the word chocolate and see where that gets you.

But all is not chocolate. One of my favorite non-chocolate desserts is pecan pie. I was introduced to this delicious Southern dessert while working in a restaurant and have not turned my back on a slice of pecan pie since. In Mexico, the birthplace of chocolate and where we currently live, we are surrounded by bakeries (*panaderías*) offering a veritable landscape of goodies, including breads, flan, churros, almond croissants, and, my favorite, Mexican wedding cookies.

As an eater, I was surprised to learn that a great divide existed between cooking and baking. Gullet-driven, I was just happy to consume whatever came out of whichever kitchen. Watching *The Great British Baking Show*, however, educated me on how baking requires an unusual skill set: a visual artist who is savvy about chemistry and anal about details, all managed and directed by a refined sense of taste. The only part of that TV show I question are the names of the experts—Mary Berry and Paul Hollywood. Are you kidding me? Quick, someone call central casting. At least their shows are always sincere and friendly, and, quite frankly, I love watching. I suspect if they had put Gordon Ramsey in charge, every show would have ended with a cake fight.

Arlene is an excellent cook but mostly steers clear of baking. Simply put, she doesn't believe it is in her wheelhouse. But that doesn't mean she doesn't make dessert. On the contrary, she makes delicious fruit pavlova, apple clafoutis, orange and Grand Marnier souffle, and biscotti, to name but a few. That's plenty of wheelhouse for me.

A Summer's Tale

Run for it, boys! It's the Grim Reaper.

The Cook

Mark, like many English majors, believes in bookend structure. We wrote about A Winter's Tale, so it just stood to reason that we needed A Summer's Tale.

So here we are.

Although I much prefer summer to winter, I like cooking in winter more than I like cooking in summer. The heat, yes, but also the foods we eat. In winter, I can make casseroles, stews, soups that feed us for many days. I can freeze some for a later time.

Not so easy in the summer.

Summer is barbeque, salads, pastas. And tacos. I have to do something with all that meat leftover from my grilling.

I love to grill boneless, skinless chicken thighs. (You have to wonder about boneless, skinless chicken things. Where does all that skin go to? Is there a factory in some corner of the world that takes all these chicken skins and makes schmalz out of them? And who buys that? Curious minds need to know.)

Once grilled, we can eat the thighs as is. Or I can make chicken tacos. Or chicken salad, which is especially wonderful during the summer. I love to add some walnuts and golden raisins to my chicken salad. Mark likes his on a bed of lettuce while I love to make a sandwich. Loving bread the way I do, it is not a surprise that I love sandwiches. Especially BLTs, which is a whole other story. There is nothing as good as a BLT in summer with fresh, vine-ripened tomatoes.

Pasta is always good in the summer. It doesn't take long to make and can be made on the stovetop, no oven required.

I make lots of pesto—a great byproduct of having basil plants. When the pesto is already made, Pasta with Pesto is basically boiling water. Lately, I've been making my pesto with walnuts rather than pine nuts. It is not about cost, really, but about walking. The store that sells fresh walnuts is closer than the store selling pine nuts. Laziness always wins! (To be fair to me, the difference in steps is double. The walk from our house to the walnut store and back is about 7500 steps. The longer walk is about 13,000 steps.)

I also make pasta with olive oil and garlic. Sometimes I add shrimp for Mark. A couple of strips of bacon and you have a poor man's—or lazy cook's—version of Spaghetti Carbonara.

One of my all-time favorites is Cold Sesame Noodles.

So much pasta, so little time.

My father worked for many years in a fruit and vegetable store. As a youngster, I spent many days in the store with him. Mostly eating peas, fresh from the pod. We always had fresh fruit in the house and I still love cantaloupe, cut into bite-sized pieces. Add some blueberries and you have dessert. My father's favorite summertime dish was sliced peaches in sour cream. Can life ever get better than that?

Salads are always great for summer cooking. Or assembling as the case may be. We love to do what we call a Mexican salad. I know. The first thing you think is Taco Salad. Wrong! This salad has many different lives, but it always includes lettuce, arugula, black beans, avocado, Monterey jack cheese and tortilla chips (slightly broken). Depending on what's leftover in the refrigerator, we add leftover cooked beef or chicken, shrimp (for Mark). We also have a side of tortillas to scoop up the salad. This is one of our favorite meals—summer or winter.

If I am feeling ambitious, I might make a Niçoise Salad. I like to do this if I have some leftover cooked fish. Salmon works very well, as does shrimp. Steelhead trout is also excellent. This is a preparation-heavy salad. Small red potatoes, green beans or asparagus, olives (very necessary), hard-boiled eggs. And whatever else you want.

But as a cook, the best thing to make when it is hot is a phone call: Take Out!

The Eater

I came of age in the San Francisco Bay Area during the Summer of Love. When I think back to that carefree, frisbee-flinging summer, I don't often think of food; instead, I think of music. I think of songs, such as "Purple Haze" and "Groovin'" and "San Franciscan Nights." And, of course, I think of patchouli incense, a lot of patchouli incense, so much incense you wouldn't believe. I recall seeing movies that summer (*The Dirty Dozen, To Sir With Love, Bonnie and Clyde*) and watching TV shows (*Gilligan's Island* and "Who says I'm dumb?" *F-Troop,* as only two examples).

A war raged on the other side of the world while social protests rocked the U.S. Young women wore halter-tops; young men let their hair grow long. Bell bottoms were *de rigueur* and shoes were optional. Everyone tried cannabis at least once but few could visualize how pot would eventually become so bourgeoisie, legal, and mainstream, the way it is today. But most of all, I recall spending time outside enjoying another endless Bay Area summer.

What I don't recall is eating. Don't get me wrong. Regardless of the season, it is my firm understanding that golfers are going to golf, painters paint, and eaters eat. I'm an eater, so I know I ate; I just don't remember what I ate or anything about the experience, such memories having long-since passed through my colon. All of which means, I am going to have to look elsewhere in my life for an opening paragraph about eating during the hot months. Sigh.

One major summer event in my family when I was growing up that always involved food was my mother's birthday, which was on July 4th. Family members would gather at my parent's house, bringing dishes to eat and alcohol to drink, like Wisemen bringing gifts to suburbia. Eventually, the men in my family would get drunk, play poker, and argue. Meanwhile, the women, as I recall unfavorably, did the dishes. *O tempora, o mores!* I am certain, if my mom had anything to say about it, she would have never been born on the Fourth of July.

Which is why my next attempt at opening this essay will fast-forward to my time in the U.S. Navy. During active duty, I was assigned to the Seabees, the Navy's construction force, where I worked as a journalist in PAO (Public Affairs Office). A typical Seabee rotation was six months in home-port (domestic) and nine months on deployment (overseas).

My last overseas deployment was to Diego Garcia, a tiny horseshoe-shaped, British-owned atoll with only 30 miles of low land in the middle of the Indian Ocean, one-thousand miles south of India and seven degrees off the Equator. Temperatures were never below 70-degrees or above 100-degrees Fahrenheit. Sand to the left of me, sand to the right. Sharp blue water extended as far as the eye could see beyond those grains of sand. A scientific expedition once tested the waters around Diego Garcia and called it "exceptionally pristine." Tall coconut trees swayed in the breeze. The only time when a day wasn't bright and sunny was when it rained. In other words, life on this tiny speck of land was always summer.

So, what did I eat? Everything. The Navy fed me four times a day! Surely, I could come up with a food story from my beachy days on Diego Garcia worthy of opening this essay. And—hold my beer--I can.

Ten of us were taking what was generously referred to as an on-island R&R. This meant we didn't have to show up for work but we couldn't leave the island; a happier version of *Papillon* without either Steve McQueen or Dustin Hoffman chewing up the scenery. On one of our R&R days, we checked out deuce-and-a-half trucks from the base motor pool for a trip to the gorgeous lagoons on the other side of the island; in addition to lagoons, the area housed an abandoned plantation, school, and hospital, remnants of a once-thriving coconut harvesting operation. As sailors, we had plenty of beer in the trucks but lacked food. We presented our provisions request for a party of ten to the chief petty officer in charge of the mess hall. In true military fashion, they gave us ten of everything: ten hamburgers, ten hot dogs, ten chickens, ten steaks. We all had robust appetites but nobody could finish ten of everything, even though we had forgotten to bring any sides.

Upon reflection, that's a pretty lame story for promoting the benefits of summer eating. Instead, I shall now stick to more recent times and talk about what Arlene makes during summer. That's easy, because summer is Arlene's fourth favorite season for cooking. If we were to eliminate grilling on the barbecue from our summer menu—an easy dismissal since we grill all-year-around, even when it's snowing—we mostly eat from four main categories during the hot months: fruits, salads, pasta, appetizers.

Since moving back to Mexico, we have enjoyed fresh fruit and vegetables, farm to tienda to our house, daily. Some of the fruits and vegetables are organic and all of what we buy is locally grown. The fruits are usually added as side dishes or as part of a dessert. The vegetables, on the other hand, often get the full Pixar treatment and are turned into ratatouille, one of Arlene's favorite dishes.

Arlene makes entrée salads, such as a Niçoise, as well as what we refer to as a Mexican salad (mixed lettuce, arugula, radish, green onion or red onion, black beans, Monterey Jack cheese, and tortilla chips, tossed with a spicy vinaigrette). She also tends to make light pasta dishes this time of year, including pesto fettucine, pasta in garlic and olive oil, and, one of our mutual favorites, a cold sesame noodle dish.

As a dyed-in-the-wool, bred-in-the-chicken-bone member of the Crazy About Deep-Fried Chicken Club, I must put a plug in for fried chicken, which, for me, is almost always finger-licking good, regardless of the source. What pairs nicely with fried chicken is Arlene's macaroni salad and coleslaw; her slaw is a delicious side based on her mother's recipe.

If we are not very hungry, we might make a basic antipasti plate with a few meats and cheeses, along with nuts (preferably roasted almonds) and olives (especially those meaty green Italian olives). Bread or crackers or both might find its way onto the platter, and sometimes homemade hummus or pesto.

When all else fails? We call a restaurant and order takeout. Hey, it's summertime and the dining should be easy.

Hunting & Gathering

I love gourmet shops but it can take two weeks
just to get enough ingredients for one meal.

The Cook

I always thought that shopping should be an Olympic event. You place a shopper in the middle of the store with a list of items to buy. The Olympic shopper who buys the most things on the list, in the least amount of time, wins the medal. This seems not to be as easy as it sounds for most people.

But I am great at it. It is a talent that I've worked hard to hone.

You could set me down in the middle of a store anywhere in the country and I can find my way out, to the bathroom, to the woman's shoe department. There is nowhere in that store that I can't get to, except maybe the Men's department, which I consider a real waste of space. Men should order out of catalogs and then stores wouldn't have to waste precious real estate on men's stuff. It all looks alike anyway.

This is very impressive for someone who has absolutely NO sense of direction. I get lost all the time. If given a 50-50 chance, I'll take the wrong turn 90% of the time. If I take the correct turn, it is pure guess and luck. I have gotten lost driving home; I forgot where I was going and just keep going. I really don't like making turns, especially left turns. I almost always turn right, except off elevators and then I'm so confused I step in one direction, then the other until I can make up my mind. And my choice is almost always wrong.

My sister and I came by our abysmal sense of direction very honestly. Both my father and my mother had horrible senses of direction. They actually got lost going to Montauk Point at the end of Long Island. I mean even I know that you just keep driving West from Long Beach until there is no more land.

Venice, Italy, is known to have winding streets that turn people around and make them lose their sense of direction. I've often thought that Venice is where I should live. It wouldn't improve my sense of direction, but everyone else would be like me.

But I digress.

Given my love of shopping, it is odd that I don't love grocery shopping. But grocery shopping is different. How life enhancing is it to buy toilet paper? Or cleaning supplies?

It's not like buying shoes, is it?

But I am learning to enjoy it a bit more here in Mexico. Shopping—at least for me—in Mexico is similar to shopping in Manhattan. I go to lots of small stores: the meat store, the vegetable store, the fish store. You get the picture.

When I lived in NYC, I shopped just about every day after work. I walked over the butcher and bought some meat, then to the vegetable guy for some veggies, maybe the cheese store. Then home to cook. My kitchen had few cabinets and no real storage. I had a small refrigerator and an even smaller oven.

I like to think that my time in New York was the training ground for my eventual move to Mexico. I feel like I have come full circle.

How cool is that?

There is a lot to love about grocery shopping—even for a reluctant shopper like me—in Mexico. Since we don't have a car—unbelievable to those in the U.S.—we walk everywhere. And that means grocery shopping. Of course, we can order from the supermarket here and get our goods delivered. And I do that for large items: toilet paper, detergent, etc. For fish, meats, cheeses, and vegetables, I prefer to shop at the small, local shops. Just like I did in New York.

The small fish shop where I go gets fresh fish every Thursday. So, there you can find me almost every Thursday. I buy enough for that night's meal. Okay, sometimes I buy extra and freeze it. But seldom.

I usually buy vegetables as I need them or maybe a day or two in advance. We get super great produce here, and I buy whatever they have fresh at the little organic market close to our house.

Just like I have a fish place, I have a chicken guy. It is a long walk—not so long, but uphill on the way back—so we don't go too often. I buy a couple kilos of thighs and breasts and freeze them.

Meats are bit more difficult here. I don't like the meats in the supermarket, so I buy most meat frozen. Good quality, but frozen. We don't eat much red meat so this is not a problem.

I guess I just like walking and do all that grocery shopping just to make it look good.

The Eater

Do you remember those life-sized museum dioramas of early man hunting and gathering dinner? If they wanted to update those dioramas for modern times and include me, it would be yours truly wandering the aisles of Costco on a Saturday afternoon, stopping to munch free samples from various food vendors. And if left unfulfilled from the small vendor portions, the next display would show me eating one of those famous Costco hot dogs, face smeared in mustard, and slurping a soft drink—all for the low-low price of $1.50 USD.

Truth be told, I am a poor excuse of a hunter or gatherer. As Exhibit A, let me tell you about the time I went clam digging.

At the time, Arlene and I co-owned with another couple a vacation house in Florence, Oregon, on the central coast and about sixty miles west from Eugene. The house was a classic Lindal Cedar-style home: A-frame with post and beam construction, an impressive wall of windows, a wrap-around deck, and so on. Our large lot was protected by a high wall of Rhododendrons. We didn't have an ocean view, but we had what I called "ocean-hear."

One Saturday when all four of us were staying at the vacation home, I had registered for a clam-digging class, offered through the local community college. Students were told to arrive at a particular estuary by nine in the morning, wearing clothes that could take a licking and keep on ticking, waterproof boots for trekking in deep mud, and a wide-brimmed hat to block the sun, just in case it made an appearance. We were also told to bring a small shovel, knife, and bucket; the latter, we were told, was not just for transporting our booty of clams but to sit on, because the instructor guaranteed we would get tired. He was right.

The estuary was at low-tide, which meant we had to slog our way through a quarter-of-a-mile of recalcitrant mud to reach our so-called "hunting" grounds. We were on the traces of soft-shell clams and were hoping to bag our daily limit of 36 by noon, when the class was scheduled to end. Fortunately for us, we were tracking soft-shell clams and not razor clams. In the Bivalvia class, soft-shell clams are the ones known for bringing down the curve. I hesitate to call these clams stupid—to generalize and offend so broadly--but when a shovel breaks the mud near them, they are more likely to treat it as a celebration, something akin to watching a fireworks display, and go ooh and ahh. They are not threatened. Razor clams, on the other hand, are extremely sensitive to vibrations and at the first felt vibration will burrow deeper with their strong muscular feet, hoping to elude capture. Razor clams know when to get the hell out of Dodge.

Nonetheless, finding and scooping soft-shell clams was still hard work. First, I had to look for holes in the mud, an indication of a likely hidden clam. If I was lucky, the clam would squirt water, further helping to identify its location. I like to think of it as an overconfident clam taunting the hunter: "Hey, dummy. Yoo-hoo. I'm over here." Once a hidden clam is spotted, I was instructed to dig around it, being careful not to crack the shell with my shovel. Which meant at some point, I had to get on my knees and dig with my hands, feeling around in the muck for the outlines of a shell. Bingo! Got one. I carefully shoveled the clam from the mud and airlifted it into my bucket; 35 more to go.

After bagging my first clam, I was already tired. But I mucked on and by noon I had 36 clams in my bucket. I had my limit, which didn't count several clams so severely damaged by my sloppy shovel technique to be rendered useless, even for steaming. The instructor gave us a five-minute tutorial on cleaning clams and back home I went, the victorious hunter.

I placed the uncleaned clams in the fridge, sat my weary body down, and ate lunch. Once refreshed, I was ready to put the finishing touches on my clam-digging and clean my bounteous booty. Now, as all good chefs know, it is important to work with sharp knives. Unfortunately, my fishing knife was deader than disco and about as dull as a speech by Mitch McConnell. The process was simple. I would hold a clam in my palm and use my knife to severe the obscene-looking muscle from the shell. Then I would insert my knife under the clam and loosen it from the shell, dealing with the neck and membrane as best I could.

It took me three hours to find and capture 36 clams, and another three hours to clean them, leaving most of those sorry-looking mollusks unappetizing on the plate. Nobody would eat my clams; even I passed after a couple of chewy, gritty bites. If a wiser mind than mine had prevailed, I would have purchased a bag of 50 already-cleaned clams for a mere $15.

Put another way, if two trains leave the station at the same time and one is going to a mudflat and the other is going to a grocery store, I'm riding the one heading to the store.

And when I get there, I'll be as happy as a clam.

The Word on the Street About Street Food

And I thought it was impossible
to ruin chocolate.

The Cook

Oh, my, where do I start with Street Food?

Watching endless food and travel shows with hosts, usually men, eating all sorts of foods from street vendors, makes me sick. Yes, sick. Just watching them. What you don't see, are the flies all around the food before and after preparation. Do you know where that fly was before it stopped on your taco? Do you want to know?

Okay, I know I'm adverse to eating food, any food, outside. Flies, bees, yellow jackets. They all land on my food. As a child I remember eating a great hotdog (Nathan's to be sure) and sharing it with a yellow jacket at the other end. I finally just gave the whole thing to the yellow jacket.

Living in New York City, I NEVER, EVER ate a street hotdog (sitting all day in murky water). Or a falafel, or a hot pretzel, or anything. Obviously, this is a long-term phobia, not one adopted in Mexico. Or Paris. Or wherever.

Cooking what is commonly known as street food is a different matter. I like to think of myself as the Queen of Tacos. I truly believe that anything tastes better in a tortilla.

My favorite taco is a chicken taco. I use the small street tortillas—you can buy them at the supermarket. I season some boneless chicken thighs (I love the Trader Joe's BBQ Rub and Seasoning with Coffee and Garlic. But, of course, use whatever you like.) and grill them, about 7 minutes each side. Chop them into bite-sized chunks. I always "cook" my tortillas in a Comal, but you can use a cast-iron skillet, lightly toasting them. Keep the tortillas warm in a clean dish towel. (Unless you are making hundreds of tacos, don't put the tortillas in the microwave to cook. It is just not as good. Trust me.)

Mix up mayonnaise with sriracha and spread on each tortilla. Put chicken thighs in the taco and top with some quick pickled red onions. (Slice ½ red onion very thinly. Add three tablespoons unseasoned rice wine vinegar, two tablespoons water, two teaspoons sugar and ¼ teaspoon salt. Mix well and put in refrigerator. You can double or triple this recipe, keeping the ratios consistent. I also use this recipe for cucumbers.)

These are the best tacos.

Of course, you can also do a taco with grilled steak. In this case, I top the steak with some shredded cheese, a bit of sour cream, and some lettuce or arugula.

Oh, I also love to do a Mexican-French fusion taco. Enclose some ratatouille in a tortilla and sprinkle some cheese on it. Pop into the microwave to heat the ratatouille (assuming this is leftover ratatouille) and melt the cheese.

And a word about hot dogs. I take my hot dogs very seriously. Buy the best you can (Nathan's, Costco, Hebrew

National, or any artisan ones you come across). As far as I'm concerned, hot dogs are only good if they are grilled. Boiling hot dogs is a disgrace to them. When I smell hot dogs grilling, I am brought back to my youth, eating grilled hot dogs on the beach. I can actually smell the ocean and feel the sand.

Proust: step aside! Remembrance is not a madeleine, but a grilled hot dog.

In writing this essay, I did a bit of research on what's considered street food to see if I've cooked any. And I have. French Fries. Fish and Chips. I've never made a Vietnamese Banh Mi, but have eaten lots of them. And pizza. Never thought of pizza as a street food, but I can see that. I've tried making pizzas, but haven't been too successful yet. My pizzas have been edible, but not great. They are a work in progress. I've eaten my share of Naan and Focaccia, but never made them. Should be fun to try.

Simply put, I love to eat Street Food. In my own kitchen, cooked by me.

The Eater

As small kids wearing Little League baseball caps and jerseys, I doubt many of us truly knew the meaning or tragedy behind the word suicide. But that is what the bravest of us always ordered for our snow cone after each game. To clarify, a suicide snow cone included a drop from every flavored syrup on the truck, leaving in its wake an unidentifiable mess that tasted about as good as it looked. What? Wait! Did I just taste lime? Or was that root beer? Cherry, anyone? In hindsight, it was as disgusting to look at as it was to eat.

But that wasn't the point. A snow cone offered a great outdoor dining experience with teammates. *Bonhomie* all the way around, all for one and one for all. And it marked the first time I encountered a food truck, what I—and many others — would eventually refer to as a roach coach.

Okay, so here's my dilemma. I like street food, but it worries me. Sometimes I think I might be the only one carrying this burden. For America as a whole, the food cart or food truck business is annually a billion-dollar enterprise. Portland, my home for thirty years, has well over 500 food carts, and all of them are organized into pods. I can't organize five of anything. So, well-done, Portland! I believe it was CNN who declared the Rose City home to the world's best street food.

People flock to urban food trucks like thirsty mammals to a watering hole. Just not me. Don't get me wrong. I've ordered from food carts before and enjoyed the experience. I especially like the aroma, as I pass a line of carts on my way to a meal someplace else with more comfortable seating.

That's because I am a cautious street food consumer. When dining from a food cart, I will almost always pick from one of two menus: Thai or Mexican. If it's Thai, give me Pad Thai every time; partly because I love Pad Thai (who doesn't?), but also because after trying so much of it over the years, on the street or in a restaurant, my body is accustomed to performing a taste challenge of its own. Will this be the best Pad Thai I've ever tasted? TBD.

If I order from a truck specializing in Mexican fare, I will invariably order a burrito, a dish, oddly enough, I never seem to order in a sit-down restaurant. There must be a logical explanation for my burrito problem, hidden somewhere in a back issue of *Psychology Today*. I hope so, because I don't understand such behavior, and I am embarrassed to own up to it. Frankly, I'm embarrassed by so many things I do, the burrito will just have to get in line and wait its turn.

Today, whenever I walk the streets of San Miguel, I am seduced by delicious smells, some from food carts, others emanating from small family-run restaurants—and all of it makes me hungry. The nose inhales; the juices flow. But do

I stop? No. It's a flaw that has kept me from enjoying many incredible food-cart meals across the planet, from Oregon to New York City to Mexico.

I suspect, deep down and without any proof whatsoever, I am concerned about the safety of the food. And I don't fully understand my concern. It's not as if an indoor restaurant with ceiling fans, plastic chairs, and generic posters would be any cleaner. If you've ever watched the TV show *Restaurant Rescue*, then you know how filthy a restaurant kitchen can get. I only have one thing to say to Robert Levine, the muscular host of the show: Put the sledgehammer down and slowly walk away.

Yes, I am an eater. But I am also a street food skeptic.

I suspect my paranoia about street food is a vestigial remnant of a generation gap. If I were thirty years younger, I imagine I'd be planning my next visit to a food cart pod and what to order, with all of the focused attention of Napoleon mapping out a campaign.

If I were sixty years younger, I'd still be eating snow cones.

Let's Do Lunch

The house salad comes with your
choice of dressing: French, Bleu Cheese,
Thousand Island, or Metabisulfite.

The Cook

In the 1950s and possibly in the early 1960s, there were the Ladies Who Lunch in New York City. Their husbands toiled away at making loads of money (*Mad Men?)* while the ladies (not women yet) lunched and shopped.

I was never that lady. Not even close. I didn't even know one of those women. But I've always been intrigued by those ladies. Okay, part of me wanted to be one of them.

When I picture these Ladies Who Lunch, I see a slim, attractive woman, wearing a hat and gloves. I know how long ago we wore those things. Personally, I never wore a hat and never owned a pair of white gloves. (I did and do own a beautiful pair of red leather gloves, but those don't count. Even though I love them.) But I can't seem to shake that picture out of my mind.

These ladies not only lunched at the expensive restaurants, but also at the high-end department stores.

Granted, I've haunted all varieties of department stores—both in Manhattan and other places—and often had lunch or a snack in their restaurants. I always feel elegant eating in department store restaurants; the better the store, the better the restaurant. We're not talking basement cafeteria dining here.

When I was young and living in New York, I would take one vacation day in late summer to buy my fall and winter clothes. I spent most of the day at my favorite store, Franklin Simon, which is now long gone. It was a small department store, with very personalized service. Franklin Simon was located on 34th Street, which at that time also had a wide array of shoe stores. (Be still my heart!)

I didn't "lunch" at that time. I was too young and self-conscious. I usually just grabbed a slice of pizza.

Later, in Portland when I was older and had more money, I always took the day off for the Nordstrom Anniversary Sale in July. Yes, I was the one at the door when it opened at 7 A.M. I always treated myself to a nice lunch. Alone. Sometimes the best way to shop and eat.

I do love lunch in department stores. It is something that Mark has learned to accept. On one of our early visits together to New York, we went to lunch at Barney's. It was fantastic. Unfortunately, I read the bill without my glasses on and left too little money. To Mark's everlasting embarrassment, they followed us out, clutching the bill. We paid, but never returned to eat there again.

Now, I've been reading about the "Ladies Who Power Lunch." Hmm. I never power-lunched with either men or women. I guess when you power-lunch, you don't drink and eat healthy looking salads. I like a glass of wine with lunch—especially now that I am retired—and something other than a salad. I think I'll skip the power-lunches.

Ladies Who Power Lunch wear expensive suits and carry fancy leather briefcases. They wear impossibly high heeled shoes. I was never that.

At some point—I don't really remember when—it dawned on me that I could invite friends over for lunch. So, the ladies who lunched became The Women Who Cooked and Ate.

Entertaining and cooking for a woman's lunch is different than cooking for a mixed group at dinner. I don't know why, but it is. For a lunch with my woman friends, I like to make something light, but elegant, that ends with a decadent dessert.

Poached, cold salmon is always good. It is elegant and can be made ahead of time. You can start with cheese and good bread and butter, or my new all-time favorite, *Gougères*. End with a drop-dead, delicious dessert and you're all set. Oh, don't forget the wine. You need a nice, cold bottle—or two—of decent white wine. I think the most important thing to remember about this kind of lunch is to do whatever you need to before the ladies arrive. You don't want to be in the kitchen cooking when the gossip starts flowing.

A few years ago, I made lunch for two friends. I was trying a new recipe as usual. If I remember correctly, it was just about the first week we got our dog, Duke. I need to say a word about Duke. He was a huge (90 pounds) Standard Poodle, apricot (we called him blonde). He was a free to good home pet and turned out to be the best dog we've ever had. His former owners loved him and took good care of him. He was very social and lovable. As we ate lunch, I didn't realize that time was passing quickly. I had forgotten to take him out for his midday pee. He came and put his head on my lap. I thought it adorable—and it was—until I realized that this was his signal that he needed to go out. How sweet is that?

(Duke died in 2019 and we miss him every day.)

Anyway, the lunch was wonderful. I made panini and oven-roasted fries. The panini was great, fresh bread, layered with Italian Fontina cheese and prosciutto. I don't have a panini pan so I just placed the sandwich on my stove-top grill pan and weighted it down with a heavy lid. It worked great.

We had biscotti for dessert.

At the last lunch I gave for friends, I made a Niçoise salad. This salad is a bit time-consuming to make, but you can do some of it day ahead and most of it the morning of the lunch.

For another lunch, I made ravioli, stuffed with homemade ricotta. It is not as difficult to make as you might think—or fear. I buy wonton wrappers since I don't have a pasta maker. Ricotta is so easy to make that you'll wonder why you ever bought it. In fact, you can make it more quickly than going to the store.

Basically, you boil whole milk (8 cups); add a cup of heavy cream, if you want, and a teaspoon of salt. Bring to about 200 degrees, almost a boil. Lower the flame to low and add 3—4 tablespoons of white vinegar, or fresh lemon or lime juice. I usually use lemon juice. Curdles will form almost immediately. Spoon the curdled milk off into a sieve lined with cheesecloth, set over a bowl. Let the ricotta drain for 15 minutes or so. It will stay fresh in the refrigerator for a few days, or you can freeze the ricotta.

How easy is that? But I have digressed.

So, to sum this all up. The Ladies Who Lunch morphed into the Ladies Who Power Lunch who morphed later in life to the Women Who Cooked and Ate. After all, a lady cannot exist on clothes shopping alone.

The Eater

Have your emoji get in touch with my emoji and let's do lunch.

Scratch that. I am going to pass on lunch today, folks. In fact, of the 23 meals I eat each day, lunch is the one I am most likely to skip. I don't actually eat 23 meals daily, to be honest, but apparently it seems that way to Arlene. Several times a day, she will shake her head and ask, "How can you still be hungry?" My appetite helps explain why my waistline looks like what architects call a rotunda. Long ago, I nicknamed my belt Magellan.

In Mexico, where we currently live, we don't often eat lunch. Instead, we continue the culinary trend of blending two meals into one. For example, breakfast and lunch are often combined around the world, resulting in the portmanteau known as "brunch." These days, Arlene and I combine a late lunch with an early dinner, most likely between 2 P.M. and 4 P.M. I have taken to calling it "dinch." (In case you hadn't guessed, I made up that word. Clever me.) That said, don't expect dinch to take the food world by storm. The meal I'm referring to already has a perfectly acceptable official Spanish name: *comida*. The bigger point, I suppose, is that lunch has dropped out of my everyday vocabulary lately, and I am struggling to find enough words to answer the topic of "doing" lunch.

Since lunch meals for me rarely happen these days, I have no choice but to enter Mr. Peabody's Wayback Machine and stop at the Catholic school I attended during my elementary and middle-school years. In spite of its draconian reputation, the school gave us time-off for lunch. What it lacked was a cafeteria. We ate at our desks, pulling smelly odds and ends from brown bags and cartoon-painted lunch boxes. The older grades, mop and bucket in-hand, would serve as first-responders in what became known as the Vomit Brigade; the younger grades giveth and the older grades taketh away. The only exception was on Thursday, when our mothers would serve us steamed hot dogs for our main dish and cupcakes for dessert. We considered it the holiest day of the week.

After I traded the limited dining opportunities of parochial school for a public high school that offered a cafeteria and an open-campus policy during lunchtime, there was no going back. You can take the kid out of Catholic school but you can't take the cafeteria out of the kid. Or something like that. Not only did I get to eat in a cafeteria, I had five or six different classrooms to go to, instead of staying in the same room for an entire day. What a concept! As a result, with the exception of self-imposed dieting to make weight for wrestling, lunch for me became a brave new world.

Then came college, with the usual lunch fare of burgers and fries and pizza. One early morning after college, I found myself on a bunk in a barracks in the U.S. Navy stationed in San Diego, rudely awakened by a drill sergeant throwing a trash can at the end of my bunk and screaming at me to get my ass out of bed. It was 4 A.M. and I was in boot camp. Because it was summer in San Diego, the day was hot, very hot. By the time lunch rolled around, I was not only starving but parched. I literally sucked the liquid out of sliced cucumbers in the chow line, savoring their refreshing moist and cold taste. The Navy, of course, served me plenty of breakfast, lunch, and dinner during my stint. The military didn't stop with three meals a day but also included a meal affectionately known as midrats, short for midnight rations. Midrats, an extra hot meal for sailors on watch and typically served from 10 P.M. to midnight, goes back to 1902 in an act signed by President Theodore Roosevelt. Since then, it has evolved to become a late-night buffet, a dining experience enjoyed by not only those on watch but those staying up late to play poker.

After the Navy, it was back to college and the usual lunch fare of burgers and fries and pizza. I met Arlene during my second, ahem, tour in higher education and the rest, as they say, is culinary history.

I was no stranger to lunch in what I refer to as my P.C. (Pre-Comida) Period. I loved a veritable smorgasbord of foods for lunch, everything from sandwiches (BLT, egg salad, corned beef, pastrami on rye, French dip, grilled cheese, grilled chicken, grilled whatever) to salads (cobb, taco, shrimp or crab Louie) to hot dishes (put a hot dish in front of me, and I am guaranteed to devour it). Among my favorite hot dishes are macaroni and cheese, and an open-faced turkey sandwich with gravy.

Getting back to my emoji, perhaps the biggest benefit of doing lunch is not doing it alone. During my work years, it was common to go out with co-workers for lunch, a bonding, of sorts, over calories. After my work years, Arlene and I would enjoy lunch at home together. Still do. At other times, we'd join friends for lunch as a couple or separately or lunch at a restaurant with just the two of us.

In doing research for my new upcoming book that will never see the light of day (*You, Too, Can Be a Smart-ass by Looking Up Sayings by Famous People on the Internet*), I came across two famous quotes about lunch. The first is from my old friend Epicurus: "We should look for someone to eat and drink with before looking for something to eat and drink, for dining alone is leading the life of a lion or wolf."

The second is from my much younger friend Douglas Adams: "Time is an illusion, lunchtime doubly so."

Five People—Dead or Alive—to Invite to Dinner

Double, double toil and trouble;
Fire burn, and espresso bubble.

The Cook

This is a standard question in any interview. Of course, I've rarely been interviewed so I've never had to publicly answer this question: What Five People would you invite to dinner?

I'm sure that some people have a well-thought-out, snappy, clever answer to this question. I do not. My brain is fumbling now as I write this. If I invited my cooking heroes, I'd be mortified to cook for them. Can you imagine cooking for M.F.K. Fisher? Or Julia Child? I couldn't do it. We'd have to go out to eat. And then I would obsess about where to go. Should I take them to a fancy place, or a trendy hot new casual place?

I'm sure whatever restaurant I selected would be having a "bad" night that night. It seems that whenever you find a restaurant that you love and you take friends there, the restaurant has an off night. It never seems to fail.

If I invited my writing heroes, I'd be just as nervous. Would M.F.K. Fisher (she does span many areas) even like Virginia Wolf? Would Virginia Wolf think that Lauren Weisberger (*The Devil Wears Prada*) is too shallow? Would

Marilynne Robinson hate Erika Jong, perhaps for no reason?

Of course, for the writing crowd, I could cook. They would be too busy sniping at one another to pay much attention to the food.

I could, of course, invite friends. But they already come to my dinner parties so this wouldn't be special. But I would invite Mark, for moral support if nothing else. And everyone likes Mark so he would be a good ally.

Maybe a mixture is the best: M.F.K. Fisher, Virginia Wolf, Richard Ford, Ruth Reichl, and, of course, Mark. But what would I cook? I know that M.F.K. would like something simple, not complicated. Just good food, prepared simply. Ruth would probably be happy with anything I made for M.F.K.. Virginia would be more interested in the conversation than in the food so I'm safe there. And Richard? I'd need something manly for him and for Mark. Simple, but manly.

Ribeye steak, grilled, with gorgonzola sauce and sautéed mushrooms. A vegetable on the side. Perhaps string beans? Some small potatoes, boiled.

Sounds good, but I would need to be in the kitchen too much. I want to be at the table, listening to the conversation—but never saying anything because I would be too intimidated.

Maybe I should order in, relieving me of any responsibility for the food preparation. Virginia and Richard wouldn't mind, but I think Ruth and M.F.K. would think me a wimp. Poached salmon would be great. I could make it earlier in the day. Men like salmon; it's not like a quiche which has all kinds of gender issues.

So that's it. Poached salmon with a small salad. Good bread and a lovely simple dessert. There you have it.

The Eater

Let's get down to business here. Who's cooking? Because I sure as hell am not making dinner for five people I don't even know. Especially if they're dead. What do you feed a dead person anyway? A zombie cruller? Ouch. That one hurt. Even I felt it.

Words do, indeed, matter, and when you deal in words, context is everything. If Arlene tells me she's going to take me out, I ask where? If an assassin says he's going to take me out, I'm running in the other direction, bobbing and weaving. If we tell friends we'd like to have them over for dinner, it means one thing. If Hannibal Lecter tells me he would like to have me over for dinner, well, that's a meal of an entirely different color, to mess with a metaphor, and one I don't want to attend, especially since I would be the *entree du jour* that evening.

As the Eater in this exercise, I expect those I invite to do all the cooking. Sorry, guys. Those are my rules and that's the context. Choke on it.

Granted, I've been known to cook a meal for the two of us, occasionally, or assist Arlene in making a meal, more

frequently, or make a special romantic dinner just for Arlene. Scratch that last one. It hasn't happened yet, although
I've considered doing it many times. And it's the thought
that counts, right? Yeah, right.

The fact remains, Arlene is a much better cook than I
am. She would have to think twice and click her heels three
times before eating a full meal I prepared from scratch.
That's why whenever I planned to do a special solo dinner,
it always seemed to make more sense to either go out to
someplace fancy — but not too fancy — for that special dinner or reheat leftovers that she expertly crafted.

To answer the question, someone will need to first tell
me who's cooking the meal. If nobody raises their hand,
then I plan to invite five of the top celebrity chefs in the
world, dead or alive, and they'll be doing the cooking. End
of story.

I searched my stomach, mind, and the internet for the
best chefs and came up with a long list. I deleted several
immediately.

Guy Fieri is out because he has too much frenetic energy, in my opinion. Although I applaud his relentless efforts
in promoting chefs and restaurants, I doubt I could keep up
with him. Besides, I don't have any tats or piercings. Alton
Brown is too nerdy and arrogant, so he's out. As is Mario
Batali, who is clearly out; Mario you were a very, very bad
boy.

I'd love to invite Hugh Fearnley-Whittingstall for
his name alone, which sounds like a character in a P.G.

Wodehouse novel. But I don't know what or how he cooks, so sayonara HFW.

I love Anne Burrell, but she can be pretty critical and could view me as the Worst Eater in America ("No. No. No. You use a spoon to eat soup. A spoon, not a fork."). She's out.

Perhaps the best thing about Damaris Phillips is her charming personality, coupled with the fact we're both Sagittarians, but I don't think her country cooking will work for me. Gone.

Then there's Robert Irvine of *Restaurant Rescue* fame. But his show has morphed into a Dr. Phil knock-off, with families pouring out coffee and their heavy hearts during his show, and featuring marriages on the brink of divorce. Sorry, I can't deal with all that drama. Adios, Robert.

After living for so many years in Mexico, I'd probably want some Mexican food, even if it has an American-twist. That could mean Rick Bayless, so he's a maybe.

I'd also want Asian food and initially considered David Chang. But, let's face it, the dude's got a potty mouth, and I wouldn't want to offend my other guests. Pack your knives, David. This is a family show.

Which brings me to Rachael Ray. She's always a perky sprig of fresh air and makes a good meal in 30 minutes, but I'm looking at a long night of eating, so I won't be inviting RR. Apologies to all your fans and to perkiness everywhere.

That's who's out. So, who's in?

Definitely Julia Child is in. She cooked French food using a lot of butter. Besides, I would love to hear her high-pitched nasal voice. Her voice alone would give me goosebumps. She's a keeper.

I'm also inviting Bobby Flay, because I've watched so many of his television shows I seem to know him and he's always pleasant.

There is no way I'm having dinner without the irrepressible and charming and outspoken Anthony Bourdain. He's definitely in.

I would love some good ol' New Orleans cooking. But I'm torn between Emeril Lagasse (just to hear him say "Bam!") and Paul Prudhomme. So, I'm putting them in my Maybe column, as reserves in case any of my invited "guests" don't show up.

I love Italian food, so with Mr. Batali out of the running, I'd invite Lidia Bastianich, the queen of Italian-American cooking. Besides, Arlene dined at her restaurant in New York and raved about her home-made pasta, which was actually made in a high-end kitchen and not someone's home.

I'm torn between inviting Julia's good friend Jacques Pépin or Wolfgang Puck. The former is a culinary institution, while the latter is a culinary empire. I'm leaning toward Mr. Puck on the strength of his name. How can you resist the combination of Wolfgang and Puck? In my opinion, Wolfgang and Puck would be a great name for an accounting firm. Undecided, I'll save those two for my backup list.

That leaves one spot open. Okay, I got it. I'm going with Thomas Keller. His reputation is stellar (hey, that rhymes:

Stellar Keller); we've even dined at his restaurants. He gets the edge, in part, because he has a famous Napa Valley restaurant, and, in part, because I lived in St. Helena on my grandparents' ranch in the heart of the valley as a kid, a stone's throw from the famous Silverado Trail.

So, when all is said and done, here's the score. My invited guest chef list includes Julia Child, Bobby Flay, Anthony Bourdain, Lidia Bastianich, and Thomas Keller. Those are the five people I've chosen to cook my dinner. My alternate chefs, with their knives packed and ready to go on a moment's notice, would be Rick Bayless, Emeril Lagasse, Paul Prudhomme, Jacques Pépin, and Wolfgang Puck. I would pick Samin Nosrat to be the moderator for the evening. Her enthusiasm is boundless, and her running bite-by-bite color commentary would be hilarious.

Best of all, I'd invite Arlene to join me for the meal. I suspect having the world's best chefs make our romantic dinner for two would go a long way toward making up for all those romantic dinners I never made.

The Authors

ARLENE KRASNER (The Cook) taught sign language to chimpanzees, composition to college freshmen, and writing to technical writers, English majors, and engineering graduate students. She worked as a technical writer, documentation manager, and an engineering manager in the computer industry. She owned a business communications company for several years. With a life-long fascination with food, Arlene has been both a recipe tester and a recipe twister. She also worked as a cook for a fraternity house (don't ask!). Through it all, Arlene has been, from first course to last, a writer, as reflected in her first book, the food memoir *Kosher Sutra*. She lives with her husband, Mark Saunders, in the beautiful colonial city of San Miguel de Allende, Mexico. *She Cooks, He Eats* is her second book.

MARK SAUNDERS (The Eater) prefers to write short pieces befitting his height and attention span. *Nobody Knows the Spanish I Speak*, his humorous memoir about dropping out and moving to Mexico, was voted a Top 3 book in San Miguel in 2012 and is being reissued in a special 10th anniversary edition. *Dogs, Cats & Expats*, his second book, was published in August of 2021. Mark is a former winner of the Walden Fellowship, awarded to only three Oregon writers or artists each year. Back in his drawing days, more than 500 of his cartoons were published nationally. His film scripts have won awards but garnered little money, while his stage plays have been performed in the U.S., Mexico, and England. His essays have appeared in Volumes I, II, and III of *Solamente en San Miguel,* as well as in online publications. *She Cooks, He Eats* is his third book.

More Knish Books

Nobody Knows the Spanish I Speak by **Mark Saunders**. A humorous memoir about what happens when an American couple in their late-50s facing the loss of their high-tech jobs choose to drop out, sell almost everything they own, and move to the middle of Mexico, where they don't know a soul and can barely speak the language. Voted a top 3 book in San Miguel. *"Nobody may know the Spanish Mark Saunders speaks, but Dios Mio, does he know how to crack wise with the best of them. Take the title. Can't read it without smiling." Jodi Lustig, Book End Babes Reviewer*

Kosher Sutra by **Arlene Krasner.** A food memoir about the author's search for a meaningful life, ill-equipped as she was at times to articulate what that truly meant. Yet when all else failed—her career, her marriage, her much-adored but silly-looking AMC Gremlin—she could always rely on her love of food, running the table from comfort food to nouvelle cuisine. Kosher Sutra is a wonderful palate cleanser that fits sweetly and nicely between the courses of Oy vey and Mazel tov. Don't just change your life... change a recipe! *"After reading Kosher Sutra, you'll think an old friend popped back into your life for a few days and feel a little miffed that she didn't stay longer."* Foster Church, Pulitzer Prize-winning author of Discovering Main Street

***Dogs, Cats & Expats* by Mark Saunders**. In this long-awaited sequel to the humorous memoir *Nobody Knows the Spanish I Speak*, which turns out not to be a sequel after all, Saunders shares his thoughts and experiences, mostly funny and a few more serious, in this collection of 30 essays about dogs, cats, and his life as a clueless expat living in the middle of Mexico. *"Don't read this book! Unless you want to laugh. Then by all means read this book! Mark Saunders offers you the unvarnished truth. Take him up on it!"* David Temple, author of Five Times Lucky (Winner of the 2021 American Fiction Award for Comedy)

Our focus as Knish Books is in two general areas of interest: food writing and humor writing. Or, as we like to say, food that makes you smile and laughs that make you hungry. Knish Books is based in the beautiful colonial city of San Miguel de Allende, Mexico, selected by Condé Nast Traveler magazine as the "Best Small City in the World." www.knishbooks.com

CPSIA information can be obtained
at www.ICGtesting.com
Printed in the USA
JSHW021148070822
28797JS00001BA/63